ANDRÉS BELLO

ANDRÉS BELLO

Philosopher, Poet, Philologist, Educator, Legislator, Statesman

by

Rafael Caldera

Translated by John Street
Fitzwilliam College, Cambridge

London
GEORGE ALLEN & UNWIN LTD
Ruskin House   Museum Street

First published in English in 1977

This Translation ISBN 0 04 920049 6

Printed in Great Britain by
W & J Mackay Limited, Chatham

Foreword

This is an exceptional book, the work of an author on the threshold of manhood – 'a chalk sketch executed in my adolescence', as Dr Rafael Caldera describes his essay on Andrés Bello – written at the age of 19 about the most universal man of letters produced by the American Continent. Rafael Caldera's book was awarded the prize in a rigorous academic contest in 1935, and in the years since then it has had the distinction of repeated editions – this is the fifth – without any change in ideas and with little re-touching since its first appearance in print. Its continuing validity fully justifies a new edition intended as much for the information of a wide reading public as for the use of students of the personality of America's leading humanist.

This truly is a book with a fortunate history, since it would be natural if a text written at 19 years of age were forgotten, even by its author, as the work of a youthful apprentice.

What is the reason for an occurrence so uncommon in Hispanic American bibliography? I think it would be wrong to attribute this event to Dr Rafael Caldera's rise to the presidency of his country. The best proof that this great literary success is not owed to this circumstance lies in the fact that the editions of this little book appeared many years before the Venezuelan election which placed in Dr Caldera's hands the direction of his country's affairs. When Dr Caldera was elected President in December 1968, this book had already gone through several editions: the first in 1935, in Caracas; the second in 1946, in Buenos Aires; the third in 1950, in Caracas, as number 37 of the Biblioteca Popular Venezolana; and the fourth, with a few changes and additions, also in Caracas, in 1965, arranged by the Instituto Nacional de Cultura y Bellas Artes for the centenary of Bello's death. In 1973 the fifth edition appeared, particularly intended to serve as a symbol of accord between the six Andean countries which signed the Andrés Bello Cultural Agreement.

I believe that the prime reason for the special success of this book is simply the opportune counsel of one great teacher:

counsel which Rafael Caldera, then a young university student
of political science, received from Dr Caracciolo Parra León, 'a
man of exceptional qualities, with a fervent love of the University
and of learning'. Caracciolo Parra advised him to approach the
unique figure of the humanist by the one true way: the direct
study of Bello's complete works. And in fact the simple explanation of the extraordinary success of the essay lies in this piece of
advice, given by teacher to pupil – although of course we should
take into account the qualities and ability of the apprentice
author, who was able to do justice to the important task which
his teacher entrusted to him. The seed fell on fruitful soil, and
the result gained the Andrés Bello prize of the Academia
Venezolana de la Lengua, in the first contest organised by that
learned society. Rafael Caldera faithfully acknowledges his debt
of gratitude to Dr Caracciolo Parra at the beginning of his books.

Early Venezuelan scholarship concerned with Bello, dating
from the Emancipation from Spain in the first quarter of the
nineteenth century, at the time when the first works of this son of
Caracas were written in London and became known at home,
was unable to undertake the task of studying the whole of
Bello's works, since these were only brought together for the
first time in the fifteen volumes of the *Obras completas*, published
in Santiago, Chile, between 1881 and 1893, thanks to the dedication of the Amunáteguis. Although admiration for Bello's work
did produce respectable results in Venezuela, there had been no
attempt to present and analyse from the whole of Bello's own
writings the great work he accomplished in a wide range of
cultural fields.[1] Rafael Caldera undertook this task with his
characteristic straightforwardness and decisiveness, 'I per-
severed, reading and annotating Bello's complete works,' he
tells us. And through this, and through Miguel Luis Amunátegui's biographical detail on Bello, he came to see the need for
'a synthesis of Bello's thought', a 'complete reappraisal', intertwined with one dominating idea: that of the 'grand humane
unity which regulated the astounding variety of his wide-
ranging work'. Such were Caldera's method and object, but he
had another firm conviction: that Bello's teachings were 'still
valid for Spanish America'. Among the civilian leaders of the
creators of the independent Spanish American Republics,
Bello's impressive stature has earned him a permanent place at

the side of the great military heroes of the movement. Caldera himself admits that it was a revelation to him to recognise in Bello a paradigm of Spanish American politics and civilisation: on the one hand, there was the intellectual liberator; and on the other, the establisher of the social, juridical and administrative norms of these new states, brought into independent life in the first third of the nineteenth century. Bello was a complete education in political humanism, not only for Venezuela but for the whole continent. It is easy to understand how a student of the pressing problems of Spanish America should reach such a conclusion, for Bello's notions showed how the new societies might be developed following doctrines based on study, reflection and deliberation. This revelation appears clearly in Caldera's work, in its 1935 form, and even more clearly in one of the few additions made in the Buenos Aires edition of 1946, from which comes the quotation with which I end this Foreword.

And so the amalgam of these three factors – the counsel of a teacher, the excellence of a method unused so far in Venezuelan work on Bello, and the ability to understand, together with the intuition of fruitful ideas (such as that of Bello's importance in the development of the continent) in a young man just past his adolescence – explains the merits of this book, which has been published repeatedly, and is here published again, for it is still valid.

Rafael Caldera divided his work into two parts. In the first and shorter one he sketches Bello's life in a few pages; in the longer second part, under the title 'The Sage' – this is how Caldera felt Bello was best described – he studies the various aspects of Bello's work throughout his eighty-four years of unflagging effort. The themes he treats occupy six chapters: 1 'The Philosopher'; 2 'The Poet'; 3 'The Philologist'; 4 'The Educationist'; 5 'The Jurist'; 6 'The Sociologist'. Always basing himself on direct, first-hand quotation, he develops, with the clarity of understanding, the most outstanding points of Bello's multifaceted work, carried out as and when the 'social need' demanded, according to the requirements of an epoch when a handful of Republics, freshly awakened to political life as independent states, had to be given meaning and direction. For this was the lodestar followed in every day of his work by our leading humanist.

Dr Caldera's book fulfils the object of acting as an 'essay which brings to the public the life, work and thought' of Bello. Now it has gone through five editions in Spanish as well as translation into other languages (French, Italian, English (partly), Portuguese, Russian, Polish).[2] So Dr Caldera's book has gone beyond the frontiers of the Spanish-speaking world and spread a message of faith in the future of Spanish America, which is the central idea of the concluding chapter:

America, our half-breed America, seeks its road with redoubled faith. . . . We Spanish–Americans are trying to discover what is our own, in order to place our destiny on a firm base.

Andrés Bello, that Spanish–American in heart and brain, gives us his life as our great example, and his thought as a signal for our ears and our conscience. To mark them, and lovingly study them, is not merely to honour him: it is also to honour ourselves, the young men of Latin America's new generations. It is to receive our legacy. It is to assure our historic responsibility to do the duty which God and our native lands – united in soul and in body – have committed to our shoulders.

The first four editions of Dr Caldera's *Andrés Bello* have affirmed the book's position as a classic work of Bello scholarship. We are convinced that this book will continue to increase in importance as Spanish America continues to realise its consciousness of its own part in and its own contribution to civilisation.

Pedro Grases

FOREWORD: NOTES AND REFERENCES

1. Pedro Grases, *Antología del Bellismo en Venezuela* (Caracas: 1969).
2. French, translated by Mme Chantal de Roquefeuil (Paris: Editions Seghers, 1972, 203 pp.); Italian, translated by Franca dal Bon Dompé, with an Introduction by Professor Giuseppe Bellini (Parma: C. E. Maccari, 1972, 307 pp.); Portuguese, translated by Maria Helena Amoroso Lima Senise (Caracas: 1973, 196 pp.); a *résumé* in English, prepared by the students of the Instituto 'Andrés Bello', of Port of Spain, Trinidad (Caracas: 1971, 9 pp.); a large section was published in Russian in the journal *America Latina* (*Latinskaya América*) (Moscow), no. 6 (November–December 1972). The Polish translation by Professor Zygmunt Vojski is in press.

Preface to the English edition

It is difficult to understand why, one hundred years after his death, there is no biography of Bello available to readers of English. For if any foreigner deserves better understanding from English-speaking intellectuals, teachers and scholars it is this son of Caracas who lived in London for nineteen years, married, lost his wife and married again in England, who studied the philosophy, law, teaching system, politics and other aspects of British culture, and who retained all his life a constant and sympathetic intellectual love for the United Kingdom.

We are speaking of the scholar who has had the greatest meaning for the Spanish American family of nations, and the greatest influence on them. The poetry of Spanish America, flowing from his pen, was born in London; and it was printed, and spread from that city, in the pages of the *Biblioteca americana* and the *Repertorio americano*, historic journals which link the life of England and the civilisation of Spanish America. His *Philosophy of Understanding*, now regarded as the most profound work in the field of philosophy to appear in South America, shows the strong influence of the thinkers of the United Kingdom, especially those of the famous Scottish school. British influence is also obvious in his wide legal knowledge particularly in his texts on international law, which were the origin of Spanish American international law. Equally strong in its influence on him was the example of the balance of freedom and authority in British political life. There are many other such British influences which he felt. It must, furthermore, be remembered that Bello appears as a leading light in many intellectual spheres. His *Grammar* is still held by authorities on the Spanish language to be the best ever written in Castilian, and one of the most important in the world. From his position as Rector of the University of Chile, of which he was the true founder, he ruled the intellectual and pedagogic life of that nation in a period which is regarded as one of the most brilliant in Spanish America. From his key position he directed Chile's foreign policy, and in the Senate and as an adviser to the government he was responsible for overseeing the formation of the Chilean civil service. He drew up a Civil Code which was taken as a model not only in Chile but also in several sister republics. Finally, in science, in literature, in serious journalism, he was the leader of a great transformation in the southernmost nation of the hemisphere.

In all these activities there was the substance of what he saw, read and learned in London, in the years from 1810, when he went there on a diplomatic mission to place before the British Government the aspirations for independence of the Venezuelan patriots, until 1829, when he travelled to Chile, where for thirty-five years he laboured at his herculean tasks. When he arrived in London he was nearly 29 years of age. He had studied in the University of Caracas. He learned English by himself, as later he learned Greek with no teacher from the books which Miranda had left behind in his London house. He had written beautiful poems, historical vignettes, important documents and profound essays on grammar. In England he threw himself into study, research, the production of texts which later were to merit the attention of the most expert specialists, in medieval literature, poetry, philosophy and jurisprudence. The British Museum archives testify to his constant attendance. In London he married, first Mary Ann Boyland and later Elizabeth Dunn, he had in London six children; and in London rested the remains of his first wife and his little son Juan. He always said that: 'London is not only the capital of commerce: in no other place is research more bold, inventiveness more free, scientific thought more profound, artistic creativity more brilliant.'

All this explains why the Banco Central of Venezuela has arranged for a complete English translation of this book, written almost forty years ago as a young man's first effort, revised since in line with the latest findings on Bello's life and work, popularised by means of several editions in Spanish, and translated into French, Italian, Portuguese and, in part, Russian. The opportunity to arrange for this English translation arose through the establishment of the Andrés Bello Fellowship at St Antony's College, Oxford, from which it is hoped we shall gain great scholarly benefits and a greater interest in the knowledge of each other in the two countries which Bello loved and to which he was firmly attached. The translator is Dr John Street of Cambridge University. I should like to thank him, also Mrs Miriam Blanco-Fombona Hood for her unstinting efforts during the publication of this edition. I hope that this little essay may serve to arouse in readers of English an increasing interest in Latin America, and a greater understanding of its mind, its culture and its great figures such as Andrés Bello, who, like Francisco de Miranda and Simón Bolívar, is a permanent link between Britain and America.

R.C.
Caracas, 18 October 1974

Contents

PART I The Man

The historical circumstance of the fortunate combination of two periods and two continents produced, out of a robust nature, the personality of Andrés Bello. He was the mature fruit of Spanish colonial culture, ripened for twenty long years in the British Museum, and in Chile he found fertile soil for his seed. The generous opportunity given to him by Chile, then in the period of her peaceful creation as a nation, presented him with a clear field for his work. With his intelligence and his character he was first-class material, and here he found his *milieu*: to aid his formation, there was the quiet filtration of a traditional way of life together with the enthusiastic acceptance of revolutionary innovations; and to spur his action there was the willingness and eagerness to learn of a newly founded society – which rejected specialisation, as do all young civilisations – and which therefore encouraged the creative talents of his genius.

Naturally this portrait of a man cannot consist solely of highlights, but the brilliance is enhanced by the play of light and shade. His personality becomes firmer and more human as we consider his innate nervousness when faced with shattering upheavals – his private anxieties in a life which at certain stages was full of misery and bewilderment, his worries that his temperament was out of tune with a long and decisive period of his life.

At one time I viewed the three parts of Bello's life as three stages in vegetable life – using metaphors drawn from the forests our literature describes: trees such as the *bucare*, the *ceiba*, or the long-living *samán*. Colonial life gave him roots, essential for all life, a base which some scorn, but which the best historical opinion requires and approves. London shaped his trunk, his robust humanism, his will toughened on the anvil of his tribulations. And Chile, his second mother-land, whose people were always cordially attentive and grateful, provided the open furrow for the fruits which ripened on the mature tree.[1]

It is impossible to understand Bello's work and thought without first understanding the man. And to do this we must survey, unhurriedly yet not in minute detail, ways in which this great citizen of the mind fitted into his *milieu* and his time or, better, into his various *milieux*, his times and his great opportunity in history.

THE MAKING OF A HUMANIST

One day towards the end of the eighteenth century a scion of Spain in the Indies, Spanish America, was born to an honourable colonial family. The day, 29 November, was the eve of St Andrew's Day, and the boy was put under the saint's protection.[2] The year, 1781, was only some two years before the birth, a few blocks away, of another son of Caracas, Simón Bolívar, with whom he was to share the leadership of modern Spanish America. It was on the threshold of the 1800s, the opening of a century which gave to the New World its special place in history. The town was Caracas, the scene of a thriving cultural development which surprised shrewd European visitors, and which made it one of the centres (Buenos Aires was the other) of greatest activity in the South America of the period.

The father, Don Bartolomé Bello, was a lawyer[3] and musician; the mother Doña Ana López, was the sister of a Mercedarian friar. The grandfather, Juan Pedro López, was, according to recent findings, perhaps the most important Venezuelan painter of colonial times.[4]

The family, members of the *petite bourgeoisie* – not much money, highly cultured, intense spiritual vocation – noted with pleasure and joy the signs of a clear, alert intelligence and diligent application to study which Andrés showed from his earliest years. The father was a minor treasury official in the Province of Cumaná, recently incorporated (from 1777) into the Captaincy General of Venezuela; his artistic inclinations were towards sacred music.[5] His loving mother helped to develop the natural tendency of his character: kindness without weakness, modesty without hypocrisy, shyness in social relationships but firmness and perseverance in his work; but above all she fostered in him his sensitivity, warm without effeminacy, later to be refined by the sharp and harsh grief which he was to suffer.

Besides the uncle who was a friar, he had a sister who became a Carmelite nun. Facing the house in which Bello was born[6] stood the monastery and church of the Mercedarians; and from these various influences he gained a sound religious upbringing, which stood firm among the currents which swirled round him, and which gave him a fixed point of reference in the studies he undertook in the stormy seas of theory.

From a Mercedarian friar, Cristóbal de Quesada, came his early grounding in the humanities, and his predilection for them. Later he entered the university and with what he called an 'old and venerable wetnurse' as a favourite pupil of Don Rafael Escalona, he went through a distinguished undergraduate career. He graduated head of the list as a Bachelor of Arts on 9 May 1800,[7] and then studied law, in which he did not take a degree since he had no interest in professional practice.

Bello met and conversed with Humboldt. Following the advice of Don Luis Ustáriz he studied French, and with the help of Ustáriz and a French grammar and dictionary, plus some notions on pronunciation given him by a Frenchman, he gained a decent command of French. Later he learned English with a grammar and a dictionary, which enabled him to read English newspapers, which in turn broadened his knowledge of English, later deepened by his long residence in London. He gave private lessons (among others, to Simón Bolívar), but the derisory profit they brought caused him to abandon them in favour of his private studies,[8] principally of law, and, simultaneously, of medicine, until his pecuniary state obliged him to sit an examination which brought him the place of Second Officer in the Captain General's Secretariat, and thus converted the student into an officer of the Crown.

In the Secretariat his work was exemplary: 'Bello was the life and soul of the Captaincy General of Caracas from 1801 to 1810,' it has been said.[9] And on the 11 October 1807 he was rewarded with the title of War Commissary. He was Secretary of the official Board of Vaccination, whose President was Governor Casas. Yet the 'civil servant never killed the scholar'.[10] He continued to read European newspapers and books, maintaining his interest in world thought. In these colonial years he produced his first attempts at poetry: 'There was no party, dinner or excursion at which he was not asked to speak improvised verses.'[11] Even before he left Venezuela he could be considered a poet of some account, as can be seen, particularly, from his well-known sonnet on the Victory of Bailén and the Virgilian Eclogue, 'Tirsis, who dwellst in shaded Tagus . . .'.

Héctor García Chuecos has shown that Bello was one of the first Venezuelan journalists. In 1809, together with Don Francisco Iznardi, he planned to start a periodical, *El lucero*, which never appeared in print, but whose prospectus was widely published in Caracas early in January 1810. He was one of the most perspicacious and regular editors of the *Gaceta de Caracas*, the first newspaper printed in Venezuela.[12] Pedro Grases confirms this, and in his valuable book[13] shows that Bello, intending his piece for the *Calendario o guía de forasteros*, printed in 1810, wrote the *Resumen de la historia de Venezuela*, which was the source of the *Compendio de la historia de Venezuela* by Francisco Javier Yanes.[14] Only Juan Vicente González, in his *Historia del poder civil*, had published even a few paragraphs of this piece of Bello's work until Pedro Grases found in the British Museum a copy of the *Calendario*, whose text was completed by another *trouvaille* made in the library of Don José Manuel Núñez Ponte.[15]

CROSSROADS OF DESTINY, 1810

The date 19 April 1810 was a crossroads of destiny, for on that day Venezuela's political future was decided and, in its own ways, the will of Providence fixed at the same time the fate of Bello, who was destined to serve no longer nor to die, in the land of his birth.

Once Independence was decided upon, Bello was called to high service in his country's new system. His honourable and honest conduct in those revolutionary times brought down upon him, later, calumnies which made his life bitter. In later years he was blamed, even by men of the calibre of Francisco Javier Yanes (who had, in the first part of his *History*, used Bello's own writings) for having delayed the revolutionary movement previous to 19 April, which was stalled because the government already knew of it. This terrible charge has been countered by irrefutable testimony;[16] but we must also recall Bello's behaviour in England, where, as Rufino Blanco-Fombona states, he remained 'faithful to his mother-land and to the Revolution, neither asking for nor accepting any aid from Spain, despite his poverty'. But there is no doubt that the most conclusive proof is the high esteem in which he was held by patriots such as Roscio and Revenga, and perhaps most of all the pre-eminent position given to Bello by the Venezuelan revolutionaries in the Supreme Junta of 1810. He was given the office of First Officer in the Department of State, the highest post after that of the Secretary of State, and documents show that he remained in this position until August 1810, when he was commissioned to be one of the delegation sent to London; and so he was senior to such famous patriots as Muñoz Tébar, 'second officer and acting first officer', and Revenga and Fortique.[17]

So Bello served as First Officer of the Department of State under the 'Junta to protect the Rights of Ferdinand VII'. His style is easily recognised in some of the most important documents issued by the Junta. And Bello went to London as Secretary of that diplomatic mission (accompanying the future Liberator, Bolívar, and Luis López Méndez) on which so many hopes were founded, and which at least obtained a benevolent neutrality from Britain, although it was not able to gain any direct British aid for the patriotic cause.[18] At that time Bello was far from believing that his absence from his country would be permanent. The document detailing the officers employed by the Junta shows that the mission was intended to be only temporary; his appointment and his place in the Secretariat were maintained, and Muñoz Tébar was merely his temporary substitute. But in fact Bello's exile from Venezuela, at only 29 years of age, was to be permanent; and the grief of his absence left a permanent scar on his patriotic heart and on his poetic sensibility. He would never again see his beloved mother, who yearned for him in her declining years. But absence from his country and his home only increased his love for them, and it is true that 'it was a heaven-sent gift for Bello that he was able to remember, in his most productive years, the love of his mother and his country'.[19]

When he left Venezuela, Bello was already a trained humanist, but in London he was able to acquire wide learning and gain the scholarly refinement which made possible his later work. But it remains true that from Caracas he brought the gist of the humanist's career and his personal style in all his cultural work:

love of study, a basic system of ideas which saw him through his long life, and a research method, a clear and well-ordered critical apparatus to bring to bear on both letters and life. From Caracas, as he himself asserted, and as no evidence exists to deny, he brought the finished version of his *Análisis ideológica de los tiempos de la conjugación castellana,* which is regarded as the most original of his works. True, it was later modified in London and in Chile, but nevertheless its inspiration and its main thesis date from Caracas. In Caracas he had already composed good poetry, although not so outstanding as the verses which, Professor Edoardo Crema maintains,[20] made him the *artistic liberator* of Spanish America. Before he left Caracas his mature judgement and power of synthesis had been revealed in his *Resumen de la historia de Venezuela.* And so Bello, despite the fruitful influence of English culture in his life, never became an English scholar, but a Latin American one. When he went to Europe he carried with him his own characteristic education, the acme of a long cultural development. And for this reason, renowned authors and painstaking Bello scholars who study Bello's life in Caracas (until recently the least known of the three stages of his life) continue to reveal new facts which bring out his character and his influence in colonial Venezuela.[21]

TRIAL BY GRIEF AND ABSENCE

After the conversations in London, Bolívar returned to Caracas,[22] whilst Bello and López Méndez stayed on. During this stage Bello came under many influences, which refined his sensibilities as much as they enlarged his knowledge and introduced him to the harsh struggle for a living. He suffered for many reasons: absence from his country and from his mother (his father died in Cumaná in 1804);[23] the straits of real poverty; the pain caused by calumny, which he suffered with true Christian meekness, even, in a poem, asking his daughter to pray 'for him whose unjust slander rends a man's fair name'; the sadness of being away from Venezuela when the men of his generation were performing epic deeds, and of feeling himself bypassed in the struggle to build a new life for his mother-land; and, as if all this were not enough, the gloomy solitude of losing his wife, made more bitter since he was left alone in a foreign land.[24]

From these troubles his character emerged all the tougher. What was already innate became in London an open vocation to learn, to build and to teach. Thinking, no doubt, of the great gifts he would bring to his country at the long-awaited moment of his return, he studied with dedication – ignorant as he was of the fact that Providence, intending him to be a true Spanish American, had marked him as a man whose rich harvest should be reaped in another land, thousands of miles distant from his own, but by history and race a member of the same family of nations.

The long years (1810–29) that Bello lived in London were years of agonising toil to earn his daily pittance, but they were also years of arduous intellectual work and learning which were a solace for his harsh life. He learned enough Greek to read Homer and Sophocles in the original; he prepared his most worthy and painstaking study of the *Poema de mío Cid*, which he finished in Chile but never saw in print, even though in 1862 the Chilean Government had ordered its publication in return for the gift of a portrait of Valdivia from the Queen of Spain; he wrote pieces on assonance, the chronicle of Turpin, the translation of the Bible, and produced many other articles. He took up once more his journalism (an activity which he renewed in Chile, and which he pursued throughout his life), bringing out the *Biblioteca americana* and the *Repertorio americano*, in which were published many of his articles intended to awaken the minds of the South American peoples. He became acquainted with such leading thinkers as Jeremy Bentham, James Mill and even John Stuart Mill, who was just a young boy when Bello first met his father. He opened his mind to the influence of English thought, as parts of his philosophy clearly reflect, without allowing it to destroy the classical structure of his colonial upbringing.

No less interesting are Bello's relations with men of Spanish background. Miranda's friendship, which gave him access to many other men,[25] and that of other Spanish or Spanish American refugees or political envoys, such as the dreadful Gallardo, the unfrocked priest Blanco White, the Colombians García del Río and Fernández Madrid, and the Ecuadorian Olmedo, urged him to further study and thought.[26] And Bello shone among these figures, as Irisarri noted in a letter to

O'Higgins: 'Of all the Spanish Americans who have been sent on missions to this capital by the new states he is the most responsible and the most knowledgeable about his duties, and besides this he has an attractive character and gives evidence of considerable learning.'[27]

Of what Bello wrote in London, it is his poems which are regarded as the most important part. His *Alocución a la poesía* and his *Silva a la agricultura de la zona Tórrida*, the latter of which has been called Bello's most polished poem, and for which Cecilio Acosta called him 'our Virgil with no Augustus, the songster of our tropic zone', have been recognised as the starting point of modern Latin American poetry. Professor Crema observes that the exile, slandered as he was, and scourged by his grief, brought forth in the refinement of poetry the desire to begin a corpus of literature native to the Hispanic American nations. As he says, Bello's Latin American precursors 'lacked precisely the one thing which formed the originality and glory of Bello; that is, the conscious thought that by writing and rhyming in that particular way and with that particular content they were opening a new era in the spiritual life of the continent, bringing artistic liberation'. To rival the deeds of his contemporaries, he took the field of letters in place of that of war: 'He aimed to be the artistic Liberator. The art of America was enslaved to that of Europe, and here was a field in which he could be the liberator. He would be one of the fighters in a war which was not the war of blood which, as a man, he hated.' And so conscious Spanish American letters were born with Bello: 'In Bello alone, what had been instinctive became conscious.'[28]

Bello was married twice in London, each time to an English bride. He married the first, Mary Ann Boyland, on 30 May 1815, and her death in 1821 left him to suffer the bitterness of widowerhood. But he was by nature a family man, and married again, on 27 February 1824. His new wife, Elizabeth Antonia Dunn, was to outlive him, and, in their life in Chile, seasoned the family evenings with her English accent and quaint attempts at Spanish words. Both wives gave him children, and his numerous descendants have played important roles in Chile: politicians, authors and artists, university vice-chancellors.[29] Some of his children died before he did, and the great grief this brought him, which he bore with true Christian patience, added in no small measure to the profound development of his mind.[30]

VOYAGE TO THE SOUTH

In London Bello gave his first services to the Chilean government. In 1822, through the good offices of his admirer and friend Antonio José de Irisarri, he was appointed Secretary to the Chilean Legation.[31] When Irisarri, 'the man whose spur-tipped pen is dipped in caustic ink', was replaced by Mariano Egaña, Bello also lost his post;[32] but the new Minister retained him as an adviser, so that he served the Legation until, offended by 'one of Egaña's tricks', he resigned,[33] although there was no definite break in a friendship which was to become close and permanent.

Bello was in dire financial straits when Don Manuel José de Hurtado, the Colombian Minister, gave him the temporary appointment of Secretary, an office which was made permanent on 8 November 1824. When Hurtado returned to Colombia, Bello remained as Chargé d'Affaires *ad interim* until the arrival of the new Plenipotentiary, José Fernández Madrid. The Government of Gran Colombia showed its esteem for Bello in various ways, one of which could scarcely have been better calculated to suit his character and temperament: he was appointed a member of the National Academy, established on 9 December 1826 in the Public Library of Bogotá.[34] On Fernández Madrid's arrival, Bello reverted to the secretaryship and applied for the increase in pay which was due to him under the law. But the increase was not forthcoming: Colombia's finances were not in brilliant shape, and indeed, as Amunátegui shows, on various occasions Bello had to pay from his own scanty savings or with personal loans the salaries of the officers of the Legation which the State left in arrears. But in 1828 and 1829 the scholar's pecuniary situation became almost desperate, for when he was given the appointment of 'confidential agent' in Paris he had not even the money to pay the fare.

Probably with the aim of finding a situation closer to Venezuela, Bello sought to be made Colombian Minister in the United States. 'Also I want', he said in 1826 to his friend Loynaz, 'to return to those countries and spend the rest of my

life there, and if it could be in Caracas I should be delighted.'[35]
He had already written to Gual on 6 January 1824:

My foremost object is to return to Colombia. I have a family, and I
feel that it would be impossible for me to bring up my children in
England, reduced as I am to my present means, which I owe to the
kindness of the Government, or rather of Sr Irisarri, but which
would be insufficient. Furthermore, it is hard for me to renounce the
country of my birth and to have, sooner or later, to go to die at the
South Pole, among the Chileans cut off from the rest of the world,
who doubtless would regard me as an outsider.[36]

Meanwhile the Chilean Government, following the advice of
his concerned friend Egaña – as previously O'Higgins had
accepted the advice of Irisarri – that it should acquire the valuable services of the Venezuelan scholar, offered Bello a firm base
for the upbringing of his family. His love for Venezuela, which
stayed with him up to the last moments of his life, caused him to
hesitate to accept the offer; but the difficulty of communications,
which led him to believe himself abandoned by his own country,
and, in particular, his care to assure his children's future, at an
age which left him no choice, induced him to take the resolution
to leave his country's service – a resolution which, as Fernández
Madrid said, 'I realised was extremely painful for him'.[37] He
wavered for a long time before he resigned himself to taking this
step, but circumstances forced him to it, and he went to Chile.
He sailed from London on the brig *Grecian* on 14 February 1829,
and landed at Valparaíso on 25 June. Amunátegui, writing
of this incident in his *Vida de don Andrés Bello*, opportunely re-
calls the verses which the Venezuelan poet wrote years later:
'Nature gives us one mother and one mother-land. . . . In vain
we try to adopt a new country; the heart gives itself but once.
The hand may wave a foreign flag . . ., and strangers call you
fellow-citizen; but what does that matter? The land of our birth
lives on in the human breast.'[38]

WAS BOLÍVAR TO BLAME?

Writing of the voyage to Chile, which separated Bello for ever
from his native land, Miguel Luis Amunátegui asserts that
Bolívar acted as if he were prejudiced against Bello because he

had not received from the scholar the lavish flattery to which he was accustomed.[39] Eugenio Orrego Vicuña, whilst praising Bolívar highly, repeats this idea, speaking of 'the Olympian indifference of a man who, having reached the greatest heights, engrossed in the greatness of his achievements and the magnitude of his almost omnipotent power, no longer has eyes for distant friends and colleagues nor time to give to their troubles'.[40] I have myself wondered whether Bello's wounded susceptibilities might have caused him, in his private mind, to make this interpretation, and perhaps Amunátegui might have heard it from his own lips. But I asked myself, was it in fact Bolívar's egotism or pride, indifference or coolness, that drove Bello to the south?

The documents which I have seen, examined with the coldest logic, do not support this interpretation. Bolívar always shows himself a friend and admirer of Bello, just as Bello was always the admirer and friend of Bolívar. And if Bolívar was not allowed by circumstances to raise Bello to the position which he deserved, it was partly because of the political difficulties which arose once Colombia became a country and her independence was assured, partly because of the slowness of communications in those times, and partly because of Bello's own rather nervous temperament, which kept him from acting directly in the stormy affairs of the Union of Gran Colombia.

That Bello manifested his eloquent admiration for Bolívar's achievements is openly shown by his poems;[41] and the fact that he did not conceal this regard appears from a letter of 21 March 1821 from Irisarri:

You may be as great a friend of Bolívar as you wish, and proclaim yourself on his side; but I, who am neither, knowing nothing of this man but his deeds, cannot believe him to be so great when he is unwilling to accept the help of men such as yourself. The position to which your patriotism has reduced you should be remedied forthwith by the General; otherwise he must be labelled inconstant in friendship and of little or no judgement in the choice of learned and virtuous men.[42]

And even in the particularly arduous political struggles in which the Liberator became engaged as soon as the heroic war was won, Bello did not hesitate to express his support, thinking, it seems, of the Bolivian Constitution. Amunátegui includes in his book a decisive letter on this subject, dated 21 March 1827, in which Bello honestly applauds 'the most illustrious of the sons of Colombia' and supports his statesmanlike aspirations in continuing 'with his customary good judgment the task of establishing the order of our countries on a sound base, which will inspire confidence and restore our wasted fields, our commerce and our income'. He writes:

Your Excellency's victories, talents and virtues have gained for you that lustre, that command, rather than mere influence, over public opinion, which alone can take the place of the venerable patina which centuries lend to the work of legislators. . . . If not all men are able to appreciate Your Excellency's lofty aims, if some believe that what they call liberty is inseparable from the forms accepted by the eighteenth century, and imagine that, in constitutional matters, the door is closed to new and great ideas, Your Excellency's magnanimity will pardon this error, and the success of your measures will dispel it.[43]

Nor was this the only letter of support which Bello sent to Bolívar. We need only quote one included by Orrego Vicuña, in which, on 21 December 1826, D. Andrés writes: 'I have recently received the reply which Your Excellency has been pleased to make to one of my letters, and I note with lively satisfaction that I have not lost Your Excellency's good opinion.'[44]

That Bolívar's admiration for Bello was sincere is proved by a letter from the Liberator to Santander dated Arequipa, 20 May 1825. We should discount in it any misleading intention, since it rather reflects a certain self-satisfaction and a defence against the accusations some made against him of being not well educated: 'My mother and my guardians did everything possible to give me a good education: they sought out for me the best tutors in our country. Robinsón [Don Simón Rodríguez], who, you know, was my tutor for reading and writing and grammar, and our famous Bello taught me fine arts and geography. . . .' His admiration was also tinged with sympathy and affection, as is shown in his letter of 21 February 1827 to Fernández Madrid: 'I beg you to convey the contents of this letter to my friend Bello, to whom I send my greeting with all the friendship and affection which I have always had for him.'[45]

What happened was that a combination of circumstances in

Bogotá and in London gave rise to the misunderstanding. Politically, Bolívar's situation was shaky. Vice-President Santander seized, together with the executive reins, control of the political scene, and exercised it in the face of Bolívar, with both firmness and cunning; and the fatal rivalry between the natives of New Granada and those of Venezuela came into being, and later was to lead to the dismemberment of Gran Colombia. In particular, Bolívar regarded as the only solution to his own poverty the rescue and leasing of the mines of Aroa, which he had inherited from his family in descent from their founder Francisco Marín de Narváez. In the business to do with the mines, which he entrusted to Fernández Madrid and Bello, Bolívar gave signs of his understandable impatience, which must have hurt Bello; whereas to satisfy Bello's desire to be given a post which was in justice due to him, Bolívar found himself faced with a difficult political situation and did not show the speed and energy necessary to take the measures which Bello's case demanded.

In London, where all that was known was Bolívar's immense glory and unlimited power, it was difficult to understand that the Hero already saw the approach of his repudiation and that he felt real anxiety about the business of the Aroa mines, in which Bello was one of his agents: mines which were the only thing of value in Bolívar's family heritage and his only source of financial support when he came to leave office. Indeed, Bolívar longed for the mines to become a source of income with the greatest possible speed, and in his impatience wrote to Fernández Madrid, in a letter which Bello no doubt saw, since he was Fernández's Secretary: 'I very much regret that Sr Bello has taken no steps in the business of my mine, for I am left in uncertainty not knowing the company's decision, since it has not told me whether it accepts the contract or not; and this silence is very hurtful to me.'[46]

But it must have been even more difficult to understand, in London, the letter in which Bolívar apologetically explained why he could not give a definite, favourable reply to Bello's requests:

I have received with pleasure your letter of 21 April; and, indeed, I am very sad at the situation in which you find yourself with regard to your position and income. I am not in charge of foreign affairs, since it is General Santander who has the executive power. Naturally, I would support any application you submit to him; but my influence with him is very weak and would gain you nothing. However I have told Revenga to write to the Foreign Secretary asking him to take a favourable interest in you.[47]

To Bello these words must have seemed the most brazen hypocrisy. But anyone who has studied the political situation of Gran Colombia at that time cannot doubt their sincerity. 'On 16 June 1827', writes Don Vicente Lecuna,

'Bolivar told Bello that he was unable to recommend his case to General Santander, and could only recommend it to the Foreign Secretary because, in fact, from 16 March the Liberator had, unfortunately, broken with the Vice-President, informing him directly, as he told Soublette that same day, that he would not reply to him nor call him friend. We recall this fact in order to point out that above-mentioned letter was sincerely written.[48]

The reply to Revenga's letter referred to here must have been the letter of the Foreign Secretary, Vergara (copied by Amunátegui himself), in which Vergara told Bolívar:

Sr Bello is excellent, will fulfil his duties very well, and should be appointed [Colombian Minister in the United States]; but since we need him at present in France, where he is very useful, I do not think we should order him to go at once to the United States. We have no one to replace him in Europe, and it would be neither helpful nor seemly if, when he had scarcely taken up his official position, we should relieve him and leave ourselves without any agent in France. Therefore, to reconcile these extremes, it would be best for Bello to be appointed Minister to the United States, but nevertheless remain in France until August or September, by which time we should have made some progress with the French government; and meanwhile a Chargé d'Affaires should be sent to North America.

After the courteous, albeit firm and well-reasoned, refusal, followed a list of candidates and recommendations for the post of Chargé d'Affaires.[49]

On the other hand, at the time the Colombian Government was distrustful of Bello's political ideas. As early as 1821, Don Pedro Gual, that serious and moderate man, sent to Revenga a copy of a letter from Bello to Mier, with these comments: 'I place in your hands a copy of part of a letter sent to Don Andrés Bello, resident in London, and since it clearly shows that his opinions are contrary to those of our system of government, I am informing you of it so that you will treat this person with the necessary reserve.'[50] In this letter, apart from expressing an unfavourable opinion of the United States, Bello, like many of the great men of the time, merely evinced his belief, in theory, in the superiority of monarchy as a system of political organisation; although he recognised that ours was 'one of those countries whose circumstances forbid the consideration of that type of government'. We shall return to this question of Bello's supposed monarchism in the last chapter of this essay; for the moment, in the matter of judging the problem of his voyage to Chile and the alleged responsibility of Bolívar for his rejection, we must note this circumstance, which explains the coolness of the Colombian Government towards Bello's requests.

Misunderstanding was bound to arise. The doubly unpleasant nature of his correspondence with Bolívar, which was in complete contrast to the previous demonstrations of affection, was so wounding to Bello that 'he feared that some enemy of his had given you [Bolívar] some disparaging report about him', as Fernández Madrid wrote to the Liberator after Bello had settled in Chile.[51] Believing himself in disgrace with the man whom he judged to be the absolute master of lives and wealth, he became desperate in his distressing situation, and felt driven to take the last resort which Chile offered him.

Fernández Madrid told Bolívar of Bello's decision to go to Chile, and the Liberator – perhaps the only one at that time in Gran Colombia who did so – fully realised the magnitude of the loss to the country if the voyage went ahead. Things would have taken a very different turn if Bolívar's letter to Fernández Madrid had not arrived after Bello had already left. In this, Bolívar wrote:

You also inform me from time to time of the wretched pecuniary situation of that Legation, which is forcing my friend the worthy Bello to leave it through sheer hunger. I do not understand how this can be, for the Treasury is constantly dealing with remittances and bills of exchange for London. They always assure me that you are being paid: but in sum this is most disagreeable and even dishonourable. Latterly three thousand pesos were sent to Bello for him to go to France, and I earnestly beg you not to let this learned friend lose himself in the country of anarchy.[52] Persuade Bello that the least bad country we have in America is Colombia, and that if he wishes to be employed in this country, let him say so, and he will be given a good appointment. His mother-land must be preferable to any other, and he is worthy of occupying a very important position in it. I am well aware of the superior qualities of this son of Caracas who is my contemporary: he was my tutor when we were the same age; and I loved him with great respect. His reserve has kept us to a certain extent apart, and for this reason I want to make friends again: in other words, to win him for Colombia.

This letter, dated Quito, 27 April 1829, only reached the notice of Bello when he was already in Chile.[53]

If Bolívar had erred by 'indifference' towards Bello, and if he did not have excuse enough in the anxieties and setbacks he suffered in his efforts to organise the newly born and already dying state of Gran Colombia, no rectification could have been more generous. When he speaks of 'reserve' he no doubt was referring to Bello's shy and gentle character, never insisting on what concerned him personally: but not even malicious distaste could find in that phrase of Bolívar's any resentment at Bello's failure to flatter him.

On the contrary the documents permit the assertion that if the Liberator had not lost the government of Colombia and then died, he would have sent to Chile for Bello, who would have found it difficult to resist his call. When he went, Don Andrés showed that he still hoped to return later to his own country. But the scholar's voyage was succeeded by the Hero's political defeat and death, and the dismemberment of Gran Colombia. These painful events, together with the sorry example of ingratitude towards the founder of the new State, must have strengthened Bello's embittered private fear of abandoning his adopted country, in which his family prospered and he was honoured, for the Calvary which must await him in his native land. Justified or not, his imagination must have contained the same thought as occurred to Juan Vicente González when he cried, in his panegyric on the death of Bello: 'The Nestor of letters was saved from the glory of martyrdom!'[54]

THE CROP BEGINS TO RIPEN

Up to 1829, by means of the good things he had written, Bello was storing up materials with which to construct his future works. He certainly continued to study after that date, for there was no surfeit of study for this man for whom 'Alfonso X's code of laws was the best digestive'; but now his reservoir of ideas needed to spill over: the flower could no longer resist its transformation into fruit. And so his life in Chile was one of constant teaching. He had taught before, but in Chile this activity (in the university, the press and public life) became his most important one, at which he worked feverishly. He taught in the Colegio de Santiago and in the Instituto Nacional, and he gave private classes; from the newspapers he prompted and directed educational advances at all levels; and he was Rector of the University of Chile from its foundation until his death.

As Senior Official in the Ministry of Foreign Affairs he was, it can be asserted, the director of Chile's international policies;[55] as a Senator and the Government's adviser, he was the nation's supreme legislator, and his Civil Code is still in force. His work in the Senate has been considered 'equally as important as his work as a jurist and educationist'.[56] He composed the most important state papers, such as presidential messages and ministerial reports, and to a certain extent is considered the creator of Chile's civil service.[57]

In Chile were published Bello's *Philosophy of Understanding* and almost all his papers on philosophy, his *Castilian Grammar* and the greater part of his *Philological Works*, his *History of Literature* and many important studies of literary criticism, a large and varied number of poems and his *Principles of International Law*.

His presence in Chile was a beneficial influence in almost all sectors of social life. He had the opportunity to discuss important social topics with men of the stature of Sarmiento, another illustrious exile, but one who had the good fortune to return and direct in his own country, Argentina, the work of recovery which he planned. Bello also engaged, with firmness and courtesy, in debates from which emerged understanding of, and insights into, complex problems; and although he met with some unpleasantness, since he was even accused of being 'a wretched adventurer',[58] his merits were appreciated and his worthy character was honoured by practically all members of Chile's distinguished society. In his old age he was an institution. A distinguished Chilean writer and diplomat paints a lively picture:

The octogenarian, fixed in his chair and walled in by books, received regular visits from his most faithful pupils and friends: Lastarria, the progressive thinker and eminent author; Barros Arana, who was planning his monumental *History*; Amunátegui, the first to undertake archival research in my country; Vicuña Mackenna, whose vivid imagination brought colour to history, life, the land, everyday things. The patriarch, unable to move about because of his age and infirmity, was also visited by 'The Most Excellent Patron of the University', as he had called President Bulnes in his inaugural speech as Rector. Montt, then President, and Varas, chief of the administration which was in power for the ten-year period 1851 to 1861, also conscientiously put in their appearances. The great scholar held out his hand to his faithful friends, whose statues have become a group in the gardens of the Library, as if to continue conversations interrupted by death: Barros Arana, Amunátegui, Vicuña Mackenna, Errázuriz, the great friar archbishop. The fading away of a great scholar and a just man.[59]

Suffering, far from harming him, purified and strengthened Bello's soul. Later, in the wisdom of his own experience in life, he wrote: 'In Providence's plan, grief is a zealous mentor which continually dissuades us from what might harm us.'[60] As his troubles sank deeper into his most intimate being, his spirit could be seen to expand into the most unselfish beneficence and the purest intellectualism. Eight of his children died before he did: one as a child, one in adolescence, and three grown men and three women; but the sorrow this caused merely purified him, brought him ever closer to Good and Supreme Truth, and increased his love of intellectual matters. In 1843, in his speech on his installation as Rector of the University, he said of literature: 'It adorned the morning of my life with sunny skies and still some rays remain in my spirit, as the flower makes a ruin beautiful.'[61] And in his *Philosophy* we find phrases like these: 'But without this mixture of pleasure and pain, virtue, the most beautiful of God's works, could not exist . . .'; 'Man's sufferings are, then, on the one hand a means of attaining perfection, and on the other a pledge of immortality. Thus divine beneficence shines even in them.'[62]

There is no doubt that in Chile he found fertile soil for his plough and for the planting and cultivation of his seed. His thirty-five long years of activity there have only merited slight criticism for his political support of the oligarchical *régime* beneath which he served. Indeed, Bello was not active in the political struggle and was a loyal servant of the government. He was even linked with Portales, who was the godfather of one of his children, and with other leading personalities of that time. But this criticism, which might have been just if Bello had been in his native country, is weakened if we take into account the fact that he was living in an adoptive country, to which it was his duty to give a system of legislation and culture, not to define political systems for it. Furthermore, his support of the government sprang from his convictions and bears no taint of flattery, but rather was the fruit of thought and good faith. With these he recognised the benefit derived for the Chilean people from 'a regular state of things, adapted to the circumstances, with a Government which maintains order and promotes improvements, and which at the same time is limited in the exercise of power by beneficial restraints which would prevent and correct abuse and lack of moderation wherever these might appear';[63] a regular order which made Chile, which a few years earlier Bolívar had called 'the country of anarchy', emerge 'the first of all the countries of Spanish America' on to the road of constructive organisation.[64]

He lived for eighty-four years. He died on 15 October 1865, after forty-five days of illness. Seven or eight years earlier he had lost the use of his legs, which had made him concentrate all the more on his intellectual work. At his death he left the Civil Code which he had been working on for thirty years full of notes introducing corrections and emendations. Among his papers were found some unpublished drafts, such as one of a new *Grammar* for use in the early years of school, which completed his revolutionary work in this field.[65] On his death-bed he raved of literary matters. Still dedicated to his work, he breathed his last.

The greater part of Bello's works was gathered by Miguel Luis Amunátegui, 'his spiritual executor',[66] in a praiseworthy collection which was published by decree of the Chilean Government under the title *Obras completas de Andrés Bello*, although regrettably this does not include his letters, his parliamentary speeches and certain other writings discovered afterwards. The collection of the *Works*, almost all of the volumes with a Prologue by Amunátegui, was first published in Santiago de Chile at the expense of the Government. The edition began in 1881, the centenary of Bello's birth, and consists of the following fifteen volumes: I, *Filosofía del entendimiento*; II, *Poema de Mío Cid*; III, *Poesías*; IV, *Gramática*; V, *Opúsculos gramaticales*; VI, VII, VIII, *Opúsculos literarios y críticos*; IX, *Opúsculos jurídicos*; X, *Derecho internacional*; XI, XII, XIII, *Proyectos de Código Civil*; XIV, *Opúsculos científicos*; XV, *Miscelánea*. In 1930 a second edition was begun under the auspices of the University of Chile and with financial co-operation from the Venezuelan Government. No changes were made in this edition, which is a faithful reproduction of the first except for the order of the volumes. Only nine volumes appeared: I, *Poesías*; II, *Gramática castellana*; III, IV, V, *Proyectos de Código Civil*; VI, *Derecho internacional*; VII, *Opúsculos jurídicos*; VIII, *Opúsculos gramaticales*; IX, *Opúsculos literarios y críticos* (the first volume of the original three on these subjects).[67] A new edition of the *Obras completas* began to be prepared in Venezuela in 1948, with the valuable collaboration of distinguished Bello scholars (*bellistas*)[68] from Chile and other Spanish-speaking countries.[69] This edition is exhaustive and systematic. The texts have been carefully revised, and much unpublished material has been incorporated. Modern spelling has been adopted, and the prologues of the volumes have been entrusted to renowned specialists, who have been asked to judge what each work represented in its time, and its validity today. The plan chosen, by order of subjects, was the following: I, *Poesías*, Prologue by Fernando Paz Castillo; II, *Borradores de poesía*, Prologue by Pedro Pablo Barnola; III, *Filosofía*, Prologue by Juan D García Bacca; IV, *Gramática*, Prologue by Amado Alonso; V, *Estudios gramaticales*, Prologue by Angel Rosenblat; VI, *Estudios filológicos I* (poetical language and metre and other studies), Prologue by Samuel Gili Gaya; VII, *Estudios filológicos II* (*Poema del Cid* and writings on mediaeval literature), Prologue by Pedro Grases; VIII, *Gramática latina*, Prologue by Aurelio Espinosa Polit; IX, *Temas de crítica literaria*, Prologue by Arturo Uslar Pietri; X, *Principios de derecho internacional*, Prologue by Eduardo Plaza; XI, *Temas de derecho internacional*; XII and XIII, *Código Civil*, Prologue by Pedro Lira Urquieta; XIV, *Derecho romano*, Prologue by Hessel E. Yntema; XV, *Temas jurídicos*, Prologue by Rafael Caldera; XVI, *Textos y mensajes de gobierno*, Prologue by Guillermo Feliú Cruz; XVII, *Labor en el Senado de Chile*, Prologue by Ricardo Donoso; XVIII,

Temas de educación, Prologue by Guillermo Feliú Cruz; XIX, *Temas de historia y geografía*, Prologue by Mariano Picón-Salas; XX, *Cosmografía y otros escritos de divulgación científica*, Prologue by Francisco J. Duarte: XXI and XXII, *Labor en la Cancillería Chilena*, Prologue by Jorge Gamboa Correa; XXIII, *Epistolario*, Prologue by Augusto Mijares.

Each volume, carefully revised, contains editorial notes by the Comisión. Also the collection contains important plates, with the title-pages of the first editions and a large number of pictures of Bello. At the time of the fifth edition of this book the volumes still to appear were numbers VII, XV, XVIII, XXII and XXIII.

Apart from the *Obras completas*, Bello's works have been published many times, and his poems are current in the schools and homes of Spanish America.[70]

PART I: NOTES AND REFERENCES

1. E. Orrego Vicuña expresses the same idea: 'Venezuela formed him. London refined him, giving him finish and spiritual enrichment. And Chile was the culmination of his life, his greatest achievements, the stage for his work, the platform for his continental influence. . . .' (*Don Andrés Bello*, 3rd edn (Caracas: 1940), p. 74.)
2. The biographical narrative roughly follows, in large part, the *Vida de don Andrés Bello* by Miguel Luis Amunátegui (Santiago de Chile: 1882). A second edition appeared in Santiago in 1962 through the initiative of the Venezuelan Ambassador, Vice-Admiral Wolfgang Larrazábal. The references are to the first edition.
3. Although Don Bartolomé Bello appears to have disliked the practice of his profession. See Amunátegui, op. cit., p. 28.
4. Alfredo Boulton, *Historia de la pintura en Venezuela*, Vol. I (Caracas: 1964), pp. 167ff.
5. Don Bartolomé Bello was a musician in Caracas Cathedral from 1774 to 1787. He was professor of plainsong in the Real Colegio Seminario about this period, and it seems that he composed sacred music. Probably his interest in music brought him some money to help to pay for his legal studies; and in his practice of law he showed some traits which came out in his son: firmness, conscientiousness, indifference towards money and strength of character cloaked in his habitual modesty. He resigned his 'place on the rostrum of the Holy Cathedral Church' after refusing to obey an order of the Chapter to enter the Choir 'since he was not wearing the clerical habit, but wore a sword', an example which his colleagues followed and justified. (Details and unpublished documents in Juan Bta. Plaza, 'Don Bartolomé Bello Músico', *Revista nacional de cultura* (Caracas), no. 39 (July–August 1943), pp. 5ff.)

6. The researches of A. Boulton show that the house of Bello's grandfather López, in which Bello was born and brought up, was situated to the north of the then Callejón de la Merced, on the south-west corner of the then Esquina de la Luneta. See Alfredo Boulton, 'El solar caraqueño de Bello', *Boletín histórico*, Fundación Boulton, no. 3 (September 1963), pp. 5–27.

7. See Dr Rafael Domínguez, 'El Bachiller don Andrés Bello', *Anales de la Universidad Central de Venezuela*, vol. XIV (July–September 1925), pp. 375ff.

8. 'One of the few who gave Bello more than soft words as a fee was Bolívar who bought him a full suit, consisting of trousers and coat of good cloth.' (Amunátegui, op. cit., p. 27.)

9. Arístides Rojas, 'Infancia y juventud de Bello', in *Estudios históricos*, 2nd series, p. 25.

10. Amunátegui, op. cit., p. 55.

11. Arístides Rojas, op. cit., p. 28, quoted by Amunátegui, op. cit., p. 61.

12. Héctor García Chuecos, *Historia de la cultura intelectual de Venezuela* (chapter entitled 'La imprenta y el periodismo'); 'Primera imprenta y primer libro venezolanos' in *Bitácora*, cuaderno III (May 1943); 'Recuerdos de don Andrés Bello' in *El Universal* (Caracas; December 1938).

13. Pedro Grases, *El resumen de la historia de Venezuela de Andrés Bello* (Caracas: 1946).

14. Republished in 1944 by the Academia Nacional de la Historia of Venezuela.

15. See Pedro Grases, *El primer libro impreso en Venezuela* (Caracas: 1950).

16. See Arístides Rojas, 'Andrés Bello y los supuestos delatores de la revolución', *Estudios históricos*, 2nd series (Caracas: 1927), pp. 36ff.; Notes by José E. Machado, pp. 313–15. Further proof provided by the testimony of Col Diego Jalón, in his *Causa de infidencia*, where he informed Bello, on 2 April, of his discovery on the night of the 1st of a rising in the Misericordia barracks, of which Bello should inform the Captain General, which he only did after a lapse of time, 'which, the witness declared, surprised the Captain General'. (Vicente Dávila, *Investigaciones históricas*, vol. I, pp. 73–4.)

17. The definitive description of the list of civil servants, the *Toma de razón*, authenticated by the signature of the Licentiate Sanz, is published by Dr Cristóbal L. Mendoza and Dr Vicente Lecuna in the Introduction to the 1944 edition of Francisco Javier Yanes's *Compendio de la historia de Venezuela*. As these scholars write, this document 'proves the complete innocence of Andrés Bello of the charges so unjustly levelled against him. The government could not possibly have continued to employ, and even to promote to a position of confidence in a mission, an officer who had betrayed secrets which might have caused the failure of the revolution which had brought it to power.' See op. cit., pp. x–xii.

18. Bello's role as a member of this mission is described, among others, by Dr Cristóbal Mendoza, in his book *La Junta de Gobierno de Caracas y sus misiones diplomáticas en 1810* (Caracas: 1936), p. 43. Here and in the following pages Mendoza analyses, in the light of the documents, Amunátegui's account of this mission's interview with the British Foreign Secretary.

19. Arístides Rojas, 'Infancia y juventud de Bello', *Estudios históricos*, second series, p. 5.

20. *El drama artístico de don Andrés Bello*, unpublished. Some chapters have been given before conferences. See *Revista nacional de cultura* (Caracas), nos 19 (June 1940), 22 (September 1940), 23 (October 1940), 24 (November 1940).

21. For example, the well-known Bello scholar Pedro Grases, who questions 'how far he had finished, before 1810, his admirable work on the romance language verb entitled *Análisis ideológica de los tiempos de la conjugación castellana*', sums up his important researches into Bello's life in Caracas in the following words: 'Of his time in Caracas we must remember that from it he rose to greater heights firstly in London, and secondly in Chile. But his mind's ability to judge and to compare dates from the solid base of his life in Caracas.' Cf. *La singular historia de un drama y un soneto de Andrés Bello*, Caracas, 1943, p. 30 and 31.

22. I wrote a longer study of this arduous London period of Bello for the Semana de Bello in 1951. See 'La incomprendida escala de Bello en Londres', in *Moldes para la fragua* (Buenos Aires: 1962), pp. 31ff.

23. Alberto Sanabria, 'Don Bartolomé Bello: precisiones acerca de su muerte', *Boletín histórico* (Caracas), Fundación Boulton, no. 6 (September 1964), pp. 33–7.

24. On Bolívar's mission, see Arístides Rojas, 'Un capítulo de la revolución de 1810: orígenes de la diplomacia venezolana', *Estudios históricos*, 1st series, pp. 291–2.

25. 'He found the Illustrious Precursor's circle helpful, and it acquainted him with many of his friends, all members of the intellectual and political *élite*.' (Orrego Vicuña, op. cit., p. 75.) He also gained much from his use of Miranda's library, although I cannot agree with Orrego's statement that this library 'for the first time put philosophical tools of high quality into Bello's hands'. This is controverted by Bello's classical education before he left Caracas, which had already given him, in large part, the outline of his future works, as Orrego himself admits.

26. See, besides the biographies of Bello, Pedro Grases's monograph *La trascendencia de la actividad de los escritores españoles e hispanoamericanos en Londres de 1810 a 1830* (Caracas: 1943). The best survey I know of the influence of the Spanish liberals of the time on the Spanish American leaders is by Fr. Manuel Aguirre Elorriaga in his important book *El Abate de Pradt en la emancipación hispanoamericana* (Rome: Gregorian Press, 1941), ch. VII, pp. 123–55. See also Vicente Lloréns, *Liberales y románticos* (Mexico: 1954).

27. 'Bello, Miranda e Irisarri en Londres', by Guillermo Feliú Cruz, in *Boletín de la Academia Nacional de la Historia* (Caracas), no. 40 (October–December 1927), p. 347. This study was included in Feliú's book *Andrés Bello y la redacción de los documentos oficiales administrativos, internacionales y legislativos de Chile* (Caracas: Fundación Rojas Astudillo, 1957). The letter, dated London, 22 October 1820, is on p. 27. Also 'Bello was the soul of the group of Spanish Americans who were in London at the time'; see Arístides Rojas, 'Andrés Bello y los supuestos delatores de la revolución', *Estudios históricos*, ed. 1927, p. 79.

28. 'Tras del Libertador político, el Libertador artístico', lecture given in the Hogar Americano de Caracas, 14 September 1940, published in *Revista nacional de cultura* (Caracas), no. 22 (June 1940), and a chapter of my unpublished book *El drama artístico de Andrés Bello*. Writing of the day Bello composed the 'Silva', Arístides Rojas says: 'From that day Bello's genius was no longer the property of one country, but belonged to the whole race which discovered America, founded a civilisation there, and taught its sons to love glory, admire beauty and worship the family.' ('Infancia y juventud de Bello', p. 33.)

29. See the family tree of Bello's descendants in Chile, prepared for Luis Correa by Guillermo Edwards-Matte, in *Boletín de la Academia Venezolana, Correspondiente de la Española* (Caracas), vol. IV, no. 14 (January–June 1937).

30. See Orrego Vicuña, op. cit., pp. 359ff. for an agreeable account of Bello's nearest relations.

31. Irisarri's private correspondence bears witness to his high esteem for Bello: 'He is most able, a man of extensive reading and much learning, and furthermore the firmness and nobility of his character make him a most admirable man.' (Letter to Joaquín Echeverría, 10 October 1920.) 'He is a true scholar, by his character and learning, and even in the patience with which he bears his poverty, equal to my own, if not even greater.' (Irisarri to his wife, 10 October 1820.) See Guillermo Feliú Cruz, 'Bello, Irisarri y Egaña en Londres', *Boletín de la Academia Nacional de la Historia* (Caracas), no. 40 (October–December 1927), pp. 334ff. Also *Andrés Bello y la redacción de los documentos*, p. 13.

32. Emilio Rodríguez Mendoza, 'Bello, el maestro inmortal', *Boletín de la Academia Nacional de la Historia* (Caracas), no. 100 (October–December 1942), p. 323.

33. Amunátegui, op. cit., p. 187. Egaña had some reason to mistrust Bello, who kept up his friendship with Irisarri, with whom Egaña's relations were bad.

34. ibid., pp. 199–207.

35. Letter to Agustín Loynaz, 13 October 1826, *Boletín de la Academia Nacional de la Historia* (Caracas), no. 51 (July–September 1930).

36. Reproduced in *Boletín de la Academia Nacional de la Historia* (Caracas), no. 48 (October–December 1929), p. 535.

37. Amunátegui, op. cit., p. 304.

38. Amunátegui, op. cit., p. 301. See *Obras completas de Andrés Bello*, vol. I (Caracas), p. 604.

39. Amunátegui's notions and the extensive narrative are in op. cit., pp. 295–311.

40. E. Orrego Vicuña, *Simón Bolívar y Andrés Bello'. Correspondencia*, p. 5. Similarly, see Orrego Vicuña's *Don Andrés Bello*, pp. 33–42 and 274–90.

41. 'In praise of Bolívar, Bello sang of the *samán* tree of the Aragua countryside, as a metaphor of his greatness. Bolívar is a *samán*, nourished with all the vigour of the tropics, whose fever burns all who touch him. The wood's grain is his spirit, the sap flows in noble judgements, the breeze which caresses its branches brings forth poetry, the sciences, the arts and letters

find shelter in its beneficent shade.' (Luis Correa, 'Andrés Bello intimo', *Boletín de la Academia Venezolana, Correspondiente de la Española* (Caracas), vol. IV, no. 14 (January–June 1937), p. 63.) In 1847 Bello wrote in *El araucano* a most affectionate note on the statue of Bolívar by Tenerani. The descriptive leaflet was sent by Juan de Francisco Martín, Bolívar's great friend and executor, to four recipients: the President of the Republic, the University, the Instituto Nacional and Andrés Bello. See *Obras completas de Andrés Bello*, vol. XIX (Caracas), pp. 195–7.

42. Feliú Cruz, op. cit., p. 93. Also *Andrés Bello y la redacción de los documentos . . .*, p. 31.
43. Amunátegui, op. cit., p. 218.
44. Orrego Vicuña, *Simon Bolívar y Andrés Bello. Correspondencia*, p. 9.
45. Dr Vicente Lecuna, *Cartas de Libertador*, Collección V, vol. VI, p. 200; Orrégo Vicuña, *Simon Bolívar y Andrés Bello. Correspondencia*, p. 26.
46. Lecuna, *Cartas del Libertador*, vol. VI, p. 309.
47. ibid., p. 312. From a letter by the Foreign Secretary, Restrepo (in Orrego Vicuña, *Correspondencia*, pp. 43 and 274) it clearly appears that it was the Vice-President who dealt with foreign affairs and was dealing with this matter about September 1827.
48. Dr Vicente Lecuna, 'Andrés Bello y Bolívar', *Boletín de la Academia Nacional de la Historia*, no. 51 (July–September 1930), p. 236.
49. See Amunátegui, op. cit., p. 304.
50. 'Una carta inédita de don Andrés Bello', *El Cojo Ilustrado* (Caracas), no. 396 (June 15, 1908), p. 362.
51. Lecuna, *Cartas del Libertador*, Vol. VIII, p. 307. This letter is dated after that of Bolívar to Fernández Madrid to which I refer in the next paragraph.
52. The situation in Chile at that time justified this description.
53. Lecuna, *Cartas del Libertador*, vol. VIII, p. 364. Amunátegui (op. cit., p. 308) is not correct when he says that Bolívar wrote this letter after he learned from Fernández Madrid's letter of 18 February 1829 that Bello had already gone to Chile. The latter had not reached him since the mail was too slow. Bolívar wrote on receipt of the news from Fernández Madrid that Bello was intending to go to Chile.
54. Juan Vicente González, *Revista literaria* (Caracas: 1865), p. 309. Egaña, in his letter recommending Bello, points out that Bello, wishing to settle in some Spanish American country, 'and foreseeing that the disorders in Colombia would probably last for a long time, prefers Chile on account of its climate and the hopes of peace it holds out'.
55. Ricardo Donoso, Prologue to the volume containing Bello's work in the Chilean Senate, *Obras completas de Andrés Bello*, vol. XVII (Caracas), p. xiii.
56. Feliú Cruz, *Andrés Bello y la redacción de los documentos*. See also Feliú's Prologue to the volume *Textos y memorias de gobierno*, in *Obras completas de Andrés Bello*, vol. XVI (Caracas), pp. xiff.
57. In his speech in the Ceremonial Hall of the University of Caracas in 1944, Dr Joaquín Fernández y Fernández, the Chilean Minister of Foreign Affairs, indicated the importance of Bello's memory in the Chilean

government offices. 'The Foreign Minister', he said, 'still works in Bello's room, which emphasises the fact that his directives are still the basis of the work of the office.' At present Bello's work-table stands in a corner of the Hall in the Presidential Palace in which the President works.

58. Amunátegui, op. cit., p. 473. He sustained an especially lively polemic with Don José Joaquín de Mora, who had arrived in Chile shortly before he did, and was somewhat jealous of his renown. But in his arguments 'he never made a virulent retort. Instead of castigating, he gave a didactic lesson.' Years later, when he was in Spain, Mora generously rose to his opponent's moral stature, when he praised Bello's Civil Code very highly. To Sarmiento, who called him reactionary, Bello replied 'as he always had done, with masterly propriety and wisdom, couched in calm and paternal phrases'. See E. Rodríguez Mendoza, 'Bello, el maestro inmortal', *Boletín de la Academia Nacional de la Historia* (Caracas), vol. XXXV, no. 100 (October–December 1942), pp. 329–30.

59. Rodríguez Mendoza, op. cit., pp. 334–5.

60. *Obras completas de Andrés Bello*, vol. III (Caracas), p. 165.

61. ibid., vol. VIII (Santiago), p. 308.

62. ibid., vol. III (Caracas), pp. 166 and 167.

63. ibid., vol. VIII (Santiago), p. 273. ('La acción del Gobierno', in *El araucano*, 1842.) The distinguished Chilean writer Don Emilio Rodríguez Mendoza, then Ambassador in Caracas, gave his valuable testimony and opinion on Bello's conduct and relationships in Chile's internal politics when, in 1942, he was incorporated as a corresponding member of the Venezuelan Academia Nacional de la Historia. Some paragraphs of his work, entitled 'Bello, el maestro inmortal', sum up his ideas. 'Sr Bello had very prudently resolved to take no sides, and this was the wisest of decisions, for his mission was national and not political.' 'Shortly after his arrival, in the midst of the upheavals and extremist experiments which commenced at the fall of the liberal authoritarianism of O'Higgins, Chile began to develop an orderly organisation. In the middle years of the last century Bello was a national personnage respected for his reliability and his loyalty to order, and since the very soil of Chile imposes the salutary law of work he worked his mines and wielded his hoe in the valleys which paint the flanks of the *cordillera* with their many colours.' Events justified his faith. There was good reason for his enthusiasm for that calm and constructive *régime* through which, as Don Emilio himself says, 'the country, so narrow that, as I have said elsewhere, it is a sort of roof overhanging the sea, had begun to grow. Barrack revolts and uprisings came to an end, and the Venezuelan humanist worked without cease and without disturbance in a study smelling of books, ink and of the coffee which his own folk sent him from Caracas, and which was served to him in a porcelain cup with a gilded rim.' *Boletín de la Academia Nacional de la Historia* (Caracas), vol. XXV (October–December 1942), pp. 327–8.

64. Bello's conduct was, furthermore, sincere. When *El araucano* was founded, its editors promised 'never to enter into political controversies', although they made the exception that 'They may at times feel obliged to defend some government measure or action; and they give this notice

so that they shall not at any time be accused of inconsistency'. But support was not unconditional. 'People have said that Don Andrés Bello was weak, and followed every hint dropped by the authorities. In my opinion this assertion is unfounded. While respecting the views of others, he always upheld his own without surrender or vacillation. His alien status removed him from the fierce political struggles and kept him apart from our domestic squabbles. Some, misunderstanding his prudence, attributed his behaviour to nervousness or submissiveness. And yet, if we go through the columns of this official newspaper, for which he was responsible, we find that on various occasions he raised his voice against actions or measures which were contrary to his sentiments and principles.' (Miguel Luis Amunátegui Reyes, *Nuevos estudios sobre don Andrés Bello* (Santiago: 1902), pp. 6, 11–12.) His criticisms of actions of the *régime* were picked up by his pupils, some of whom were passionate partisans of one or other of the political parties, although this never reduced in the slightest their respect for their teacher.

65. Andrés Bello, *Gramática castellana*, unpublished work edited with Prologue and Notes by Miguel Luis Amunátegui Reyes (Santiago); published in *Obras completas de Andrés Bello*, vol. V (Caracas), pp. 311–428.

66. Note by the University of Chile in the second edition (Santiago: 1930).

67. I cite the first edition as *Obras completas de Andrés Bello* (Santiago); the Caracas edition I cite as *Obras completas de Andrés Bello* (Caracas). Bello's texts collected in the *Obras completas* are the basis and guide of my work, especially in the second part.

68. The word *bellista* is to be incorporated in the *Diccionario de la Real Academia Española* through the initiative of the Comisión Editora de las Obras Completas de Andrés Bello.

69. The Comisión Editora consisted of: Julio Planchart, Director; Augusto Mijares and Rafael Caldera, Members; Pedro Grases, Secretary. From December 1948, because of the unfortunate death of Julio Planchart, I became the Director. Enrique Planchart, who became a Member on the death of his brother Julio, also died, in 1953. The memory of these two distinguished authors and fervent admirers of Bello has constantly inspired the Comisión in its labours.

70. A great deal has been written about Bello. A fairly complete idea of the bibliography of studies of Bello, prepared by Pedro Grases, can be found in no. 4 of the journal *Cultura universitaria* (Caracas: November–December 1947), pp. 209–30. A more complete version of this appeared in no. 172 of the *Revista nacional de la cultura*, edition commemorating the centenary of Bello's death (Caracas: November–December 1965).

PART II   The Sage

Introduction

What we find most impressive when we review Bello's work is its fine intellectual balance and its exhaustive learning. He was an exemplary man. His understanding was clear and swift, his memory exact, strengthened by intense exercise; his imagination was lively, though disciplined, his sensitivity exquisite, but tempered by reason; his will calm and deliberate, bold in the struggle against the effect of social inertia in holding back progress, and tenacious in its perseverance for many years in his arduous and dedicated work.

He was blessed with extraordinary talents, fully developed within the harmony which is the reflection of nature, and, sure master of philosophy, he was able to think accurately in the most varied fields of learning.

He was not merely a scientist or a man of letters. He was a wise man, a sage, a scholar. He remembered the classical figure of the greek 'sophos': not because he knew many things, but because he was the consummate example of complete learning; because he knew the inner truth of things, felt the responsibility of one who knows his own worth; because with unquenched enthusiasm he plunged deep into the knowledge of life and used his experience to direct his pupils; and also because he lived according to the pattern of the supreme Science, and was good, and felt the close unity of the trilogy formed by Truth, Goodness and Beauty.

Bello worked from the firm base of a philosophical education, his intellect methodically developed in search of the Supreme Truth and his aspirations fixed on Absolute Good. It is easy to understand how Bello, instructed by his reading of the best authors and endowed with great talents, was able to master satisfactorily in his studies problems of very diverse natures.

Bello had a classical education, but not classical in the mistaken sense of isolation from all progress and of dogmatic belief in trivial pedantic details. It was classical in the classical sense, if I may use that expression: the study of human nature, deducing from it certain fundamental principles which govern all inquiry; the ordering and disciplining of human life, the respect for the lessons of teachers, the addition of new knowledge to old in recognition of the fact that the intellectual world is in constant evolution. This idea of the union of tradition and innovation stands out more clearly when we remember that many of his contemporaries attacked Bello as an innovator, whilst others stigmatised him as a reactionary.

Philosopher, poet, philologist, jurist, educationalist, sociologist: each is one aspect of a brilliant whole, the complete scholar. Blessed with that profound learning for which the universe is a harmonious union and all branches of knowledge are intertwined and become one, Andrés Bello is as much a scholar when he codifies Chilean law as when he sings, in a simple poem, written in some lady's commonplace book, which reveals the harmony of his soul, or enthusiastically praises the introduction of vaccination.

Bello's harmony and fine balance are the core of this essay. Perhaps it was the particular contrast with what we see about us today which gave me the idea of studying Bello as a whole, like a diamond, each of whose facets gives value to the whole, but which is of value as a whole. As we read them, the words which Bello spoke at his installation as Rector of the University of Chile seem like a definition of his own personality: 'All the human faculties form one system, in which there can be no order and harmony without the presence of all. If I may express it so, not one single fibre of the soul can be paralysed without all the other fibres degenerating.'[1]

Bello the scholar, the man who in his life gave evidence of a culture which was complete, harmonious and ordered, becomes apparent to us as we look at his most important characteristics. For Bello was a philosopher who zealously and enthusiastically cultivated the field of philosophy, marching steadily and firmly into the storms of the different schools and developing a body of ideas which reflects his remarkable maturity, preserves his living influence and even brings out the panorama of the ideas of his age. He was a poet who captivates us not only through his work but also by his idea of beauty and art and by the subtlety of his critical sense. As a philologist he was a revolutionary and a creator, a restorer and conservator, at one and the same time, of the linguistic unity of Spanish America; he was a great master of linguistic science, with his clear ideas on the birth and evolution of language and his fervent zeal for its purity, tempered by a desire not to exclude from the language forms which could enrich it. He was an educationalist who dedicated most of his life to teaching and developed clear ideas on educational problems and a disciplined system of education. He was a jurist who, modestly, laid down the clearest bases of the juridical organisation of Spanish America in both internal and international law. In sum, as a thinker he was in the closest touch with the problems of history and of life and one who, therefore, cannot be fully understood without an examination of his social and political ideas.

Bello's many-sided work was possible, very largely, because of a sociological phenomenon which has frequently been discussed. Nations progress towards their full development along the road of specialisation. The increase of progress and of population demand the formation of *élites* specialised in smaller and smaller fields of activity or research; and this brings out the cry to find in the fundamental unity of human knowledge some remedy for the deformation of the human spirit which might result from this walling in of every specialist in his particular 'field'. On the other hand, young and unformed societies reject the development of specialisation. They demand ability and understanding in various human activities from every brilliant man among them. Social reality imposes such latitude on them for the interpretation and solution of very complex problems: our keenest brains must make their mark by their capacity for synthesis.

When the time came for Bello to bring forth fruit, he was forced to launch into the most varied tasks. He published his *Cosmography* at the same time as he was busy drawing up a Civil Code. But what was special in him was that, because he was a humanist and genius, in all his works he performed well above mediocrity. For example, his *Principios del derecho internacional* arose out of the need to produce a book from which the Spanish nations could be taught; and they were published modestly under the author's initials only. For over a hundred years the test of criticism has brought out the undeniable value of a work which perhaps would not have been published in Europe, because in a more developed society a man would have been forced to choose one single field (perhaps philosophy, or philology?) outside which he would not have been allowed the authority to write or speak.

Bello's journalistic activities, for example – which stimulated a great part of his writings – reveal the characteristic needs of Spanish America. He became a journalist for those young peoples which needed instruction on Spanish America's natural wealth, culture, history, and on the great problems common to all humankind. First as editor of the *Gaceta de Caracas*, then, in London, of the *Biblioteca americana* and the *Repertorio americano*, and later, and most importantly, as the dogged editor of *El araucano* in Santiago de Chile, from that journal's foundation in 1830 until 1853, he played the role of the true journalist who, like the orator in ancient Greece and Rome, had to direct and instruct. He was not the man for unproductive day-to-day news, the sort of work which constrains the masses to take some particular view or secretly leads them astray; but in his journalistic work he must be the teacher, calm and kindly, criticising books and plays, encouraging and correcting, giving the facts and interpreting them in a moral and Christian fashion. He always had a clear view of journalistic ethics: 'If the true aim of journals is to disseminate instruction and to show men the most obvious means to gain prosperity, the honest writer should carefully avoid all the arts of deceit and seduction and limit himself to providing his fellow-citizens with sound information.'[2]

So it is not surprising that Bello's writings deal with very diverse subjects: from astronomy, physics, botany, geography, zoology and chemistry to philosophy, history, politics and sociology. For example, I should be guilty of prolixity if I catalogued all his scientific works; but I would not wish to leave the reader without some idea of that prolixity. It will be sufficient to quote a paragraph from Amunátegui's *Vida*, concerning the *Repertorio americano*, which only came out from 1826 to 1827:

Don Andrês Bello also wrote a section entitled Miscellaneous, which included short articles on telescopes, steam, blood, the magnetic needle, kidney stone, river navigation, meteorology, digestion, the source of platinum, the poisonous honey of Uruguay, wild men, the origin of cassava, the rattlesnake, the cultivation of coffee in Arabia, the milk tree, the falls of the Vinagre River, the chemical analysis of the milk of the cow tree, *huitia* in Cuba, the yellow snake of Martinique, the poisonous sap of the *ajuápar*, the age of trees, the bread-fruit tree, the heights of mountains, the gold and platinum mines of the Urals, the temperatures of man and of different species of animals, the shape of the earth, the essential oil of a South American tree, the damage caused by a blazing whirlwind, the earthquakes of 1826, the physical causes of madness, the cure for yellow fever, rain and floods in the Canary Islands.[3]

If the reader has had the patience to read this list – and reading it aloud and all at once would need a very deep breath – he will have noted Bello's particular interest in Spanish America and the use he made of it even in his unfinished medical studies in the University of Caracas.

I should not dream of asserting that Bello was a genius in astronomy or chemistry, zoology or mathematics, nor should I wish to represent him as infallible in his own most special fields, philology and literature. I should never declare that I consider Bello as the equal in philosophy of Kant or even of Cousin. I do not wish to give the reader the impression that for me Bello is a matchless oracle. But it is impossible to approach the vast scope of his work without awe. It is undeniable that he must have been possessed of some deep and magnificent human essence to enable him to be outstanding, as he was, in poetry, law and grammar, to write philosophical essays of undoubted worth and, at the same time, to undertake with masterly simplicity the most diverse themes for the instruction of the Spanish American peoples.

Far be it from me to pretend, setting myself up as the master's teacher, to judge in what Bello was successful and in what he was in error. I shall present his ideas as I have found them in his works, trying to place them within their own historical context. Before I could do this I had to make a rough sketch of the scholar as a whole, on which other brush-strokes and colours will make the portrait clear. It is this impression of grand completeness and harmony which prevails in our view of him. Great intellects such as those of Marcelino Menéndez Pelayo, Cecilio

Acosta and his pupil Barros Arana have also remarked on this, as did Bello's contemporaries Irisarri and Egaña, whose efforts when they were diplomatists in London were decisive in persuading their Government to invite Bello to Chile.[4]

Bello's 'select classical education' and 'profound knowledge' of various disciplines (Egaña), his 'wide reading and extensive knowledge, trustworthiness and nobility of character' which mark him out as 'a true scholar by virtue of his character and knowledge' (Irisarri), his 'astounding facility for assimilating the most heterogeneous and varied knowledge' (Barros Arana), his grandness which made him 'comparable in a way with the ancient patriarchs', builders, poets, philosophers and law givers (Menéndez y Pelayo), all these things make of Bello, 'the man who knew everything' (Cecilio Acosta), the complete and human scholar, the Sage *par excellence* of Spanish America.

Let us see, then, by an examination of his main facets, how the admirable and dynamic balance of his great scholarship becomes apparent.

INTRODUCTION: NOTES AND REFERENCES

1. *Obras completas de Andrés Bello*, vol. VIII (Santiago), p. 306.
2. ibid., vol. XV (Santiago), p. 65: 'La centralización y la instrucción pública'.
3. Amunátegui, op. cit., p. 242.
4. Irisarri's opinion is clearly evinced in his private correspondence (see p. 42, n. 31). Egaña introduced him to his Government in these words: 'His select classical education, profound knowledge of literature, complete command of the most important ancient and modern languages, experience of diplomacy and his excellent character highlighted by his modesty, not only render him able to fulfil very satisfactorily the duties of senior official, but his merits also would justify the Government's preference to him as against others who apply for the same office'. (Amunátegui, op. cit., p. 299.)

1 *The Philosopher*

The basis of Bello's multiple activities had to be a well-constructed and profound philosophical foundation. In a way, when we call him scholar we indirectly call him philosopher, in the sense that he held in his mind the roots of all human knowledge; but even if we think of philosophy as a specialised discipline, here too we may find in Bello an interesting figure.

In philosophy Bello never attained the revolutionary and creative importance which would have made him leader of a school of thought, as he did become the leader in Spanish American poetry and in grammar for Spanish Americans. He was too modest to take upon himself the creation of a new system of philosophy, and was too deeply convinced of the cardinal truths of classical philosophy to adopt an iconoclastic attitude. But this did not prevent him from expounding a very personal analysis in connection with particular philosophical problems, reflecting a profound and well-thought-out view of the various powerful influences which he underwent and bringing to philosophy original conceptions which foreshadowed some later achievements of modern philosophy.[1]

It was Menéndez y Pelayo's opinion that Bello's *Filosofía del entendimiento* (the first volume of a Treatise on Philosophy that was never completed) was 'without doubt the most important work of its kind in Spanish American literature'.[2] This opinion has been ratified more recently by the philosopher José Gaos: 'For in the history of thought in the Spanish language the *Filosofía del entendimiento* is the most important manifestation of Spanish American philosophy, influenced by European philosophy before German idealism and by modern philosophy up to positivism – I can prove my point – and is therefore an outstanding landmark in the whole history of Spanish thought.'[3]

Without a sound philosophical background, Bello could never have attained such stature and breadth of learning.[4] Anyone who reads his works must of necessity form the same opinion, even before he studies the strictly philosophical part. This part consists of: the *Filosofía del entendimiento*; articles on the *Filosofía fundamental* by Balmes, whom he describes as 'deservedly the most popular writer and perhaps the most learned and profound author of whom Spain can boast today';[5] studies on Rattier's *Curso de filosofía* and Jouffroy's *Teoría de los sentimientos morales*, and, incidentally, his university speeches and various others of his numerous works of criticism.

THE INDELIBLE IMPRINT OF HIS TEACHERS IN CARACAS

Bello's philosophical ideas reflect the shape of classical philosophy. Although touched by new developments, mainly in psychology and logic, his classical education shows through more clearly as he reaches the fundamental principles of philosophy. It becomes evident that the training he received in Caracas accompanied him throughout his long life as something characteristic and his own.

On the road from the New World to the Old, and from the northern to the southern hemisphere, the prints of his teachers in Caracas are clear to see. In the peaceful evening of colonial times Bello's sharp appetite for knowledge met the decisive influence of men whose thought and system gave him an enduring direction.

The first and most exceptional of these men, and the one whose influence was perhaps the greatest because it was the earliest, was the friar Cristóbal de Quesada. According to the story which Bello told Amunátegui, he was a Mercedarian friar who ran away from his monastery only to return and dedicate his life entirely to religion and study. Normally he did not teach, but Bello's uncle, brother Ambrosio, succeeded in arousing his interest in the boy, whose talents were beginning to be revealed.[6] Brother Cristóbal started him off in his classical studies with such strict discipline that he made him postpone his entry to the university until he had perfected his Latin. He directed Bello until his death in 1796. Bello told Amunátegui that he considered that Brother Cristóbal was 'a teacher such that few equal could be found at that time in all the length and breadth of Spanish America, as he [Bello] said to me when he was recalling the events of his youth'.[7]

It seems that the influence of Don José Antonio Montenegro, a priest and Bello's first university teacher, had little lasting effect on the young undergraduate; but that of Don Rafael Escalona, the disciple and successor in learning of Marrero – who introduced modern philosophy into the University of Caracas – was great. Escalona taught him philosophy until he graduated as Bachelor of Arts. Amunátegui writes: 'Don Andrés Bello always retained the warmest memory of the help which he had been given by the priest Don Rafael Escalona. When Carlos Bello went to Venezuela in 1846, one of the charges he received from his father was that he should visit the old philosopher.'[8]

THE CROSS-CURRENTS OF DIFFERENT INFLUENCES

The strength of Bello's early training becomes apparent when we consider the variety and power of the influences he underwent. His reading of modern authors, without any doubt already begun in Caracas (Caracciolo Parra-León has brought out documentary proof of the presence of the works and knowledge of modern philosophers in the old University of Santa Rosa of Caracas), became voracious in London and was maintained in Chile to the end of his life. To trace step by step the labyrinth of those influences would require a work of immense scope, limited to the field of his philosophical notions. But we can obtain some idea of the influences from a list of the authors who are most frequently named in the course of his philosophical studies.[9] By naming the most familiar we can give an approximate idea of the influences which attracted him.

The most surprising thing, for those times, is the scarcity of quotations of the Encyclopédistes. From Voltaire, some of whose plays he had translated in Caracas, there is only one quotation, on the existence of God.[10] He does not mention Rousseau in connection with serious problems, but only in anecdotes which show his familiarity with Rousseau's life, such as when he talks of the special way that bells affected him, of his shrewdness, or of his memories of childhood, when he is studying psychologically the phenomenon of attention.[11] He once speaks of D'Alembert as an 'illustrious philosopher'.[12] The name of Descartes appears only once in the *Filosofía*, and then in a very unfavourable light when he calls him so deluded 'that he maintained that animals are machines devoid of sensitivity';[13] but on the other hand, many of those mentioned are followers of Cartesian philosophy: Malebranche, Leibniz, Samuel Clarke and Hume take turns with each other in the pages of the *Filosofía del entendimiento*.[14]

Kant is also there (how could he not be?) among Bello's quotations, and particularly in the question of judgements, and their division between analytical and synthetic, empirical and *a priori*, a classification which he accepts with some reservations.[15] But the idealist with whom he seems to be on most familiar terms is 'the perspicacious Berkeley, Bishop of Cloyne', whose concept of divine influences being the cause of sensations he came to believe since it was difficult to refute it philosophically, although this concept caused him to make a public confession of faith and reject Berkeley's idealism as being contrary to Catholic dogma.[16]

He quotes Bacon in Latin, and will only accept Bacon's anathema on final causes if 'what is meant is that the end does not produce the means', because 'that is a proposition which no one can doubt'; but he utterly rejects it 'if it is claimed that there are not really any ends and means, but only causes and effects, that the eyes were not made for us to see, but that we see because we have eyes'.[17] The name of Hobbes appears several times.[18] Locke, whose *Essay Concerning Human Understanding* Bello had chosen as a text when he was learning English,[19] is also frequently quoted: at times Bello censures him as when he points out his error 'in confusing with the sensations ideas of relationships, which are products of intellectual activity, concepts of pure reason', and at others, more frequent, he defends him or bases himself on Locke's arguments.[20] He is also familiar with Condillac, and accepts him in part, but firmly rejects his error in 'making all the operations and faculties of the soul consist only of sensation'.[21] The writers of the Scottish school are well known to Bello, and their works have left many traces in his psychological and logical constructions; the names of Reid, 'the illustrious leader of the Scottish school',[22] Dugald Stewart[23] and Thomas Brown[24] are without any doubt those which most frequently meet the eye of the reader of the *Filosofía del entendimiento*. Cabanis also appears,[25] as do Destutt de Tracy[26] and John Stuart Mill, whom he knew as a child in London, whose father he knew quite well, and whose denial of free causes he rejects.[27]

Bello also shows great familiarity with the writings of the 'illustrious French philosopher' Victor Cousin, leader of the eclectic school.[28] He quotes the *Leçons de philosophie* of Laromiguière, whom some consider an eclectic and even the precursor of Cousin.[29]

The Greek philosophers are few: Plato only appears once,[30] as does Pyrrho, whom he mentions in order to distinguish Berkeley's theory from 'the ravings of that ancient philosopher who doubted everything', although 'probably no philosopher ever professed such an absurd doctrine, and that of Pyrrho was not perfectly understood by the ancients, as that of the Bishop of Cloyne has been badly understood by the moderns'.[31]

Bello's allusions to Aristotle and the scholastic philosophers deserve a separate paragraph. I shall transcribe these allusions in order to present a complete idea not only of Bello's *Filosofía*, but also of his other works. Bello's admiration for the Stagirite is evident from them, but also there are many derogatory phrases condemning the scholastics and 'the finicky niceties of the Aristotelian-Thomist doctrine' of which he speaks in his letter to Gual, criticisms levelled against the exaggerations with which, as time passed, this doctrine had been overloaded. In his *Historia de la literatura*, he says:

Aristotle was blessed with the greatest philosophical genius. A profound thinker and shrewd observer, he exiled imagination from his works. He embraced all the branches of learned research which had been known up to his time, and there was none which did not owe great advances to him. He invented the ingenious theory of the syllogism, laid down the first system of logic, created natural history; his metaphysics, the first attempt at a new science, is still worthy of study; his politics, although it does not go back to first principles, is full of admirable maxims and observations. In his ethics shine forth ideas which are as delicate as they are sound concerning the nature of man, set out with a simplicity which is at times sublime.[32]

When Bello is studying mathematical method he quotes Aristotle in the Greek.[33]

I give great importance to the study of inductive reasoning, which is useful in experimental sciences, and that of criticism, which weighs evidence or interprets unclear texts. Nor do I carry my admiration for modern things so far as to regard with scorn the heritage of that great genius who with such sagacity traced the path of reason in some of its most familiar processes. I am not ashamed to think that the Aristotelian theory of reasoning deserves study; in this subject, as in others, use should not be confused with abuse. . . .[34] The scholastics were mistaken when they claimed to give us the universal instrument of human reason with their syllogisms.[35]

Allusions such as these are repeated in various articles,[36] but all are summed up in the following comment, referring to the habit of dedication to a single intellectual discipline, immediately after he had condemned the exclusivism of mathematics: 'From this point of view scholastic philosophy is much worse, being reduced to using the syllogism as its only tool and lost in subtle abstractions which do not, as does mathematics, have any application either in natural sciences, social sciences or the arts.'[37] The scholasticism which Bello portrays here deserves his bitter criticism, though it does not apply to the philosophers of the classical Golden Age. He never quotes Saint Thomas among his sources; which is not surprising since most of the men of science of Bello's time knew scholasticism only through the criticisms which were made of it during the school's degeneracy, and they did not study Thomist doctrine directly.

Many of the authors named were Bello's contemporaries, and they enjoyed then more than they do now solid prestige and recognised authority. So we must admire all the more the firmness and clarity with which his early tutors must have taught him to evaluate modern currents and instilled the first principles in him, which emerged untouched in the difficult struggle. And we are driven to the conclusion that the milk of his 'ancient and venerable wet-nurse', the University of Caracas,[38] admirably strengthened his receptive faculties.

Bello's reiterated condemnation of empiricism is worthy of special mention. In his installation speech at the university he stated:

But even though encouraging practical applications, I am very far from believing that the university should take as its motto that mean-spirited one *cui bono?* and should fail to appreciate at its true worth knowledge of nature in all its various departments. Firstly because in order to guide practice correctly, it is necessary for the understanding to reach the culminating points of science, and the appreciation of its general forms. No doubt the university will not confuse practical applications with the manipulations of blind empiricism. And secondly because, as I said before, the cultivation of the contemplative intelligence which lifts the veil from the secrets of the physical and moral universe is in itself a positive result of the greatest importance.[39]

Having sketched the background, let us turn to Bello's doctrine. Let us see how his philosophical thought, influenced at some points by the currents of idealism, and at others inspired by the sensualists, is at root classical.

A SHORT INCURSION INTO HIS PHILOSOPHY

Bello divides his philosophy into two parts: the first, the philosophy of understanding, comprises mental psychology and logic; and the other, moral philosophy, consists of moral psychology and ethics.

At first sight there is a striking similarity between this division and Kant's pure reason and practical reason, and Kant's influence on Bello was great. The division is based on the idea that 'all philosophical notions which are not psychological should be expounded after the psychological notions' because 'the principle should precede the consequences';[40] and so he is obliged to distribute metaphysics 'in mental psychology and logic', and to give 'in the form of an appendix that which seemed to me less closely linked with the science of human understanding'.[41] Therefore questions such as the existence and attributes of God are treated in an appendix.

The way the *Filosofía del entendimiento* deals with metaphysics is evidence of a certain subjectivist tendency in it, which draws Bello into the question of the ruling principles of knowledge: ontology, he says, 'is in large part psychology itself', since 'the basis of ontology is the analysis of thought in its primitive materials' and 'principles are a property, an element inseparable from the mind'.[42]

The method which Bello follows in his *Filosofía* is the one he proclaims in it: neither based entirely on reasoning nor on empiricism. 'Philosophy in all its branches, like physics and chemistry, is a science based on facts gathered by observation and which demonstrative reasoning fertilises.'[43] Regarding the actual plan of the work, its editor writes: 'Sr Bello intended to write a textbook for the subject of philosophy in the Instituto Nacional; but his studies of the various philosophical questions took him too far, and he wrote a masterpiece because of the importance of the problems he deals with and the profundity with which he handles them.'[44] The result of this was a work which had the characteristics of a teaching textbook, as the author intended (in quotations of other authors there is, in most cases, no mention of title and page), but which because of its depth and extent was not appropriate for teaching, not only nowadays but also at the time when it was published. And so I believe that the usefulness of the study of this book is that it reveals Bello's philosophical basis, fundamental for the understanding of his intellectual activity, and, secondly, that it portrays the state of philosophy in the mid-nineteenth century by the traces we find in the mind of an able man, sensible and as unbiased as any man could be of the various schools then struggling for dominance in this intellectual field.[45]

Bello's system of judgements shows the influence of fideism, mixed with reminiscences of the tenets of the classics. The struggle between his own intimate convictions and many of those upheld by men whom he admired as great masters led him to distrust evidence as the universal and ultimate criterion of truth. 'We believe, however,' he says when he is reviewing Balmes's *Filosofía fundamental*,

that the whole search for the reason for first principles and the logical bases of the confidence we place in them, is nothing but plunging into a sphere which is beyond the possible reach of the human faculties. Our understanding is forced to believe that there is certainty, and that there are means of reaching it and truth, or else it can believe in nothing, think of nothing, even its own existence. To inquire whether there is certainty, and on what it is based, is *ipso facto* to admit the first truths and the general rules of logic without which it is undoubtedly impossible to take one step in this inquiry or in any other.[46]

In formal logic, Bello starts off from the existence of 'principles inherent in the human reason and without whose means it is impossible to make use of the understanding and conduct oneself in life';[47] and, springing from these principles, his construction in the technical subject of reasoning is classical although displaying modalities of his own.[48]

With respect to the methods of the sciences in general, he makes this clear construction: for pure mathematics, pure deductive method;[49] for the sciences which study 'intellectual, moral and material nature', inductive deductive and analogical method.[50] In the philosophical sciences, therefore, observation and demonstrative reasoning;[51] in physics, chemistry and biological sciences, observation, experimentation, generalisation by empirical reasoning, reasoning and analogy, deduction from the formulae obtained by analogical synthesis and confirmed by experience.[52]

'I DO NOT KNOW WHETHER RELIGION OR LETTERS ARE SLANDERED . . .'

In the field of metaphysical ideas Bello stands out as the religious philosopher who said at his installation as Rector of the University of Chile: 'I do not know whether religion or letters are slandered by those who think that there could be some secret antipathy between one and the other.'[53] His *Teodicea*, developed especially in an appendix to his chapter on the relationship between cause and effect, is uncontaminated by any heterodox intrusion. God is the first or prime cause, the cause which is not the effect of any other cause: all things existing outside him are the product of an absolutely free volition of his omnipotence. Bello's statement on the proofs of the existence of this prime cause shows his innermost conviction.[54]

Bello's idea of the attributes of God also makes his orthodox conviction evident. Lack of limits to space, eternity, 'infinity'; supreme intelligence, will free, sovereign and creative (*creatio est productio rei per imperium*), necessary of absolute necessity, omnipotent. God is unique, unlimited. 'He sees all as if he were present.' 'He needs no instruments for the exercise of his intelligence.' 'He perceives intuitively substances and the forms of substances, and the forms of minds and matter.' 'He is not only the principle of order, but the very pattern of the perfectness of order'; 'absolutely just, truthful and beneficent.' 'He takes pleasure in spreading life and happiness.'

This same entireness of belief runs over in the lyric feeling of the verses he composed as the introduction to his poem *América*, which was to comprise his famous *Silvas*:

But who can count the varying, innumerable total of thy great works, Eternal Cause and Source of being and of life? No man has the power to sound the deep abyss, not those pure spirits who serve as a footstool to thy throne, and hide their faces with their wings before the canopy of glory in which, sublime, thou art seated; nor those who move through limitless space, or limited only by thy sight, the immense chain which binds the worlds. All things sing the miracles of thy magnificence; thou didst unite order with richness, the simple with the varied. But man, like an insect which is born, lives and dies in the green cup of a flower, only contemplates a part of so many marvels, and in the book of Nature can only decipher one line, and adore thee.[55]

In his psychological constructions Bello starts from the existence of the human soul, intelligent,[56] free[57] – liberty which is not opposed to divine prescience[58] – and immortal.[59]

And starting from this idea he demonstrates the unity and identity of self;[60] he upholds consciousness, which is not a sense, and which is affected by all the modifications of the soul, 'although the perceptions leave no trace in the memory except when we linger a little on them', and although there may be 'sensations which are too fleeting and weak for the consciousness to seize them and memory to recall them', which is undoubtedly true;[61] he admits the magnificence of the definition 'which makes reason consist of the faculty to conceive relationships', and points out that the gravest defect of the theory of Condillac – who believes that 'sensation is the whole soul, consciousness is one of the senses – is 'that of making all the operations and faculties of the soul consist of the single fact of sensation'.[62]

EVEN ANIMALS HAVE AN IMMATERIAL SOUL

In Bello's psychology all cognitive functions, even the sensitive ones, are embraced by the soul.[63] 'Thus', he concludes, 'those who have attributed sensitivity to the body and intelligence to the soul have been gravely mistaken. The phenomena of sensitivity are modes of which we have intuition, no less than we have those of judgements or reasoning, and in all the

phenomena of which we have intuition the soul perceives itself
as a being which is always identical.'[64] From the concept of
sensation as a function of the soul alone derive conceptions such
as that 'the word idea signifies image',[65] and also other peculiari-
ties in his nomenclature and explanation of cognitive phenomena,[66] and, from this too, comes certainly his distinction
between true ideas and idea-symbols, 'which take the place of
others which we are unable to form;' that is to say, 'in which the
imaginative representation does not correspond to the object'.[67]

This led Bello to attribute to animals an immaterial soul, although one that was mortal and incapable 'of moral ideas'. He
went so far as to attribute to them 'a sort of intelligence in which
sensitivity enters as one of the elemental faculties, in the same
way as it does in ours, but sensitivity alone is not capable of the
intellectual acts of which we have intuition in ourselves'.[68] He
adds:

The dog would suffice to prove that the phenomena of intelligence
in animals cannot be explained by sensitivity alone: the dog, which
understands and obeys our orders; in which, as in ourselves, need
and danger develop marvellous cunning and sagacity; qualities
which it owes not to blind instinct but to experience, that is, to observation and reasoning, since it acquires these qualities gradually, it
learns them, it becomes educated.

Bello's attitude towards instinct is correlative to this, for instinct,
although it 'is not born of experience', relates, with respect to its
variation and evolution, to intelligence together with experience.[69] One of the psychological problems which he resolves
from an empiricist standpoint is that of general ideas. 'We
believe', he says, 'that we have general ideas which represent to
us something which is uniformly repeated in all the individuals
of the genus, when in fact we only have ideas of individuals,
ideas of individual similarities and ideas of names.'[70] This
notion, linked logically with the confusion between idea and
image and with his concept of idea-symbols, leads him to regard
as simple abstract nouns those of space, which for him is simply
coexistence, and of time, which is simply duration,[71] and even of
cause, which, he affirms, 'is nothing but the constant succession
of two particular phenomena'.[72] Regarding the idea of substance, the only thing Bello has given us is the affirmation that

the principle of substantiality is of absolute necessity;[73] together with the thought that we cannot know this substance in itself, since 'to be exact, we do not perceive any other substance but that of the individual self, and that serves us as a pattern from which to imagine the substance which, through an instinctive and irresistible analogy, we attribute to other intelligent and sensitive beings'.[74]

If we cannot know in fact any other substance but the self, we are forced to conclude that 'we do not know what are material and material qualities in themselves and not merely as causes of sensations, nor is this knowledge accessible to the mental faculties with which we are endowed', and so, after making a very full exposition of 'the question relative to the real existence of bodies' (although in his opinion 'it is completely futile'), Bello affirms that the problem of whether the cause of our sensations is really material, or whether, as 'the protestant Berkeley' maintains, it is a matter of divine influences exercised upon us, is unsolvable philosophically. He makes this philosophical idea the occasion for an avowal of his Catholic faith, not only when he says, in his *Filosofía*, 'But although strictly Berkeley's theory could be admitted as a supposition possible in the eyes of philosophy, it is undeniable that it is contrary to some of the most essential dogmas of catholicism and of almost all Christian Churches', but also, and more strongly, in his review of the *Filosofía fundamental* of Balmes in which he rejects Balmes's criticism of idealism, when he affirms:

Reason without revelation has no means of deciding whether it prefers the materialist system (that is to say, in general that which recognises the substantial existence of bodies) to the idealist system or vice versa. . . . We say reason without revelation because the catholic dogma of transubstantiation openly contradicts idealism. . . . We regard the idealist system as a false hypothesis, because it is contrary to catholic dogma, but one whose falsity cannot be demonstrated by reason alone.[75]

SOUND MORALITY, BASED ON RELIGION

Bello never wrote the *Filosofía moral*, which was the second part of his division of philosophy, and which he subdivided into moral

psychology and ethics. But some concise ideas on the fundamental problems of ethics are contained in his philosophical
writings.

In his *Apuntes a la 'Teoría de los sentimientos morales' de M.
Jouffroy*, Bello attempts to reconcile rational morality with
utilitarian morality and the morality of sentiment, convinced
of the practical correspondence of good with the absolute
interest and with the highest sentiments of man. In this Bello
yet again reflects his eclectic, harmonising temperament.

With respect to moral psychology, we have seen that he
recognised that the soul is free and immortal: immortality
which can be deduced from the need for some sanction beyond
the grave, and liberty which is the indispensable requisite for
the existence of virtue and crime.

Bello's ethic is profoundly religious: God is the basis of 'moral
order, whose laws have been stamped by the Creator on the
conscience and the heart of man'.[76] His profession of faith, his
opinion that education and the arts (see the later chapters 'The
Poet' and 'The Educationalist') are subject to moral order, and
the fundamental ideas I have just explained, show Bello always
convinced of the existence of a moral order which rules all our
actions, which emanates from God and whose prop and guide
is the catholic religion. Christianity is the obvious background
to propositions such as that 'virtue implies temptations, struggles,
painful hardships, sacrifices',[77] and that 'pain, in the design of
Providence, is a zealous mentor, which continually dissuades us
from what might harm us'.[78] The following sentence sums up
his moral conviction firmly based on religion, and is the guide-
line of his fruitful work: 'Morality (which I do not separate
from religion) is the very life of society.'[79]

CHAPTER I: NOTES AND REFERENCES

1. 'And if a large part of Bello's philosophical ideas belongs to his present
   and his past, and therefore only to our past, another part, and not a small
   one, appears in him as a glimpse into the future, as ideas in the state of
   embryonic germs, which only in our own time have found the environ-
   ment necessary for them to become fully present, completely developed.'
   (J. D. García Bacca, Prologue to the *Filosofía del entendimiento, Obras
   completas de Andrés Bello*, vol. III (Caracas), p. xii.)
2. Menéndez y Pelayo, *Obras completas*, vol. II (Madrid: 1911), p. 365.

3. Andrés Bello, *Folosofía del entendimiento* (Mexico–Buenos Aires: 1948), Introduction by José Gaos, p. xxxiv.

4. For example, the philosophical basis of his *Gramática* has been noted. 'The *Filosofía del entendimiento* comes nowhere near attaining the well-deserved fame and rich harvest that his *Gramática* gave, gives and will continue to give. But the *Filosofía del entendimiento* forms the basis and background of the *Gramática*, and being a background it has remained in the half-light, if not in the shadows.' (García Bacca, *Obras completas de Andrés Bello*, vol. III (Caracas), Prologue, p. xiv.)

5. ibid., p. 617.

6. 'As you know, from my youth I have cultivated the humanities,' he wrote in a letter to Gual from London, 6 January 1824. See *Boletín de la Academia Nacional de la Historia* (Caracas), no. 48 (October–December 1929), p. 535.

7. Amunátegui, op. cit., p. 7.

8. Amunátegui, op. cit., pp. 20ff. Amunátegui says of Montenegro that, according to Bello, he was 'a man of some worth, who wrote verses not only in the language of Garcilaso but also in that of Virgil, who had some knowledge of French literature and in his younger days had even read prohibited books; but as he got older he went back to his outdated ideas, of which he was one of the most stubborn defenders' (op. cit., p. 14). One day when he found Bello reading Racine he said to him: 'What a pity, my friend, that you have learned French!' (op. cit., p. 16). But he must have been an eminent man in his time, according to Baralt, who called him 'the good, affectionate, learned Doctor Montenegro' (quoted by Menéndez y Pelayo, op. cit., p. 357) and especially according to the university Senate, which declared in 1825 that it had seen 'with great pleasure that the tutors continue the advance begun particularly by Doctor José Antonio Montenegro, one-time Professor of Grammar and Eloquence (1788–1792), who moved a century forward in his knowledge of the young and the method of leading them gently and properly in their educational careers, and who left Venezuela the most precious memories and the most interesting present in the method he followed of uniting honour and harshness sometimes when without the latter some youth, abandoning himself to the ardour of his age, might have fallen' (*Libro de Claustros, 1799–1843*, f. 164 v, Archivo Universitario, quoted by Caracciolo Parra-León, *Filosofía universitaria venezolana 1788–1821*, p. 160.)

Details concerning Marrero and his disciple Escalona can be found in the same book by Parra-León, pp. 54–67.

9. I limit myself to authors expressly and repeatedly quoted, without mentioning all those named in the *Filosofía* and other studies, such as Fichte, Jeremy Bentham, whom he called 'the leader of the utilitarians' (*Obras completas de Andrés Bello*, vol. III (Caracas), p. 548), and those whose presence is implied but who are not mentioned by name.

10. C'est le sacré lien de la société,
Le divin fondement de la sainte équité,
Le frein du scélérat, l'espérance du juste
Si le ciel, dépouillé de son empreinte auguste,

Pouvait cesser jamais de le manifester,
Si Dieu n'existait pas, il faudrait l'inventer. (O.C. Caracas, III, p. 157).

11. *Obras completas de Andrés Bello*, vol. III (Caracas), pp. 352–3.
12. ibid., p. 393.
13. ibid., p. 486.
14. ibid., pp. 531, 160, 162, 190, 530.
15. ibid., pp. 164, 190, 383ff. In an article on international law in ibid., vol. X, p. 487, he wrote: 'The most illustrious philosophers of our times, the Kants, the Dugald-Stewarts, the Reids, the Cousins, etc.'
16. ibid., vol. III, pp. 177, 209, 269, 288, 292, 363ff., 538, 579, 640.
17. ibid., pp. 502, 504ff.
18. ibid., pp. 129, 139, 142.
19. Amunátegui, op. cit., p. 32.
20. *Obras completas de Andrés Bello*, vol. III (Caracas), pp. 120ff., 139ff., 147, 269, 287–8, 382.
21. ibid., pp. 265, 266, 267, 269, 454ff.
22. ibid., pp. 23, 114, 138, 199, 204, 208ff., 288, 289, 296–7, 316, 369, 395, 396ff., 499–500, 528, 537ff., 542ff.
23. ibid., pp. 311ff., 366, 389ff., 397ff., 446, 470, 494, 500ff., 525ff.
24. ibid., pp. 27, 57ff., 177, 214, 329, 330, 333, 334, 349, 455ff., 538ff.
25. ibid., pp. 200, 263.
26. ibid., pp. 177, 238ff.
27. ibid., pp. 149–51.
28. ibid., pp. 34, 120, 121, 138ff., 379, 383ff.
29. ibid., p. 56, n.
30. ibid., p. 187.
31. ibid., pp. 365–6.
32. *Obras completas de Andrés Bello*, vol. IX (Caracas), p. 73.
33. ibid., vol. III, p. 464; also in his articles on grammar he quotes Aristotle's *Politics* in Latin: ibid., vol. VI, p. 336.
34. ibid., vol. VIII, p. 384: speech on his installation at the University of Chile.
35. ibid., p. 418.
36. ibid., p. 491; also vol. III, pp. 140, 187, 622 n. See also, for example, *Obras completas de Andrés Bello*, vol. IX (Santiago), pp. 213, 285, etc.
37. *Obras completas de Andrés Bello*, vol. III (Caracas), pp. 528–9.
38. Letter to Pedro Gual, 1824. *Boletín de la Academia Nacional de la Historia* (Caracas), vol. XII, no. 48 (October–December 1929), p. 535.
39. *Obras completas de Andrés Bello*, vol. VIII (Santiago), p. 313.
40. *Obras completas de Andrés Bello*, vol. III (Caracas), pp. 443–4.
41. ibid., p. 7 n.
42. ibid., p. 460.
43. ibid., p. 461.
44. *Obras completas de Andrés Bello*, vol. I (Santiago), p. vii.
45. The importance of the *Filosofía del entendimiento* in Spanish American philosophy has recently been reassessed in favourable terms. To understand its present worth see the Introduction by José Gaos to the edition published by the Fondo de Cultura Económica: Andrés Bello, *Filosofía*

del entendimiento (Mexico. 1948); and the Introduction to Bello's philosophical works for the edition of the *Obras completas de Andrés Bello* (Caracas), by J. D. García Bacca. This brings out many unsuspected present-day aspects of Bello's philosophical thought. García Bacca is also preparing a book, *Introducción a la filosofía a través de la 'Filosofía' de Bello*.

46. *Obras completas de Andrés Bello*, vol. III (Caracas), p. 620. Concerning certainty and its origins, the following quotations display Bello's ideas so clearly that no commentary is necessary: 'The faith we have in our own judgements is called certainty, and is of different kinds and degrees.' 'Absolute certainty is that which we have in those judgements which involve necessary proportions of absolute necessity.' (ibid., p. 406.) 'There are two things which produce absolute certainty, evidence and demonstration.' (ibid., p. 409.) There is also physical certainty, 'but however great physical certainty is, it will never have the force of absolute certainty' (ibid., p. 411), since 'the constancy of physical laws is not of necessity absolute' (ibid., pp. 411–12). The causes of error are general or special. The general causes 'can be reduced to these seven headings: predispositions and organic states; predispositions and moral states; intellectual habits; faults of memory; lack of imagination; abuse of symbol-ideas; looseness in language, from which it follows that the same word can be understood in various ways by different individuals, and not infrequently by the same individual on different occasions' (ibid., p. 522). The special ones are sophisms or fallacies, which 'can be reduced to two classes: one alters the bases of judgement; the other vitiates the deductive power' (ibid., p. 533).

47. ibid., p. 370. The idea he has of these principles shows his tendency towards fideism, for he says that they are 'certain instincts which, when generalised, later become principles, primary laws which preside over all the acts of the intelligence' (ibid., p. 378); and that 'it is undeniable that there are in the understanding a large number of judgements and cognisances which are logically anterior to experience, which are not logically derived from it, even by some later deviation, because there can be no experience which does not imply them' (ibid., p. 383).

Among these principles he mentions: the principle of stability of the laws of nature, which he calls empirical, 'not because it is so, but because the generalisation of all empirical results is based on it' (ibid., p. 378); that of contradiction, 'a principle which is not only beyond the reach of observation, but is also necessary of absolute necessity for all judgements, all reasoning, all cognisances' (ibid., p. 379); that of causality which, according to his theory, 'is born spontaneously in the understanding because that is the will of the author of Nature' (ibid., p. 144 n.). 'Another universal principle of absolute necessity is that of sufficient reason, which we can formulate in this way: there can be nothing which has no reason for being.' 'The principle of substantiality is also of absolute necessity.' (ibid., p. 380.)

48. 'Reasoning is an act of understanding in which from one or more judgements we deduce another judgement.' (ibid., p. 421.) 'In all reasoning

the understanding takes one step, and unless it goes astray by adopting without consideration a premise or deducing an illegitimate consequence, it acquires a new cognisance.' (ibid., p. 464.) See Bello's ideas on reasoning, the classes of reasoning and his theory of the syllogism (ibid., pp. 431, 422, 472, 480).

49. ibid., p. 461.

50. ibid., p. 472.

51. ibid., p. 462.

52. ibid., p. 480.

53. *Obras completas de Andrés Bello*, vol. VIII (Santiago), p. 306. This text can be found in Pedro Grases, *Antología de Andrés Bello*, 2nd edn (Buenos Aires: 1964). In the Caracas edition of the *Obras completas* this speech will appear in vol. XVIII, not yet published.

54. *Obras completas de Andrés Bello*, vol. III (Caracas), pp. 156ff., 502ff., 133.

55. Drafts of poems, *Obras completas de Andrés Bello*, vol. II (Caracas), p. 19. On the projected poem *América* see Prologue to this volume by Father Pedro Pablo Barnola, pp. xviiiff.

56. 'The psychological formula of reason is the faculty to conceive relationships, the intuitive faculty we might say, but whose acts should not be confused either with sensation or with mere intuition, in which the soul limits itself to the contemplation of an affection of its own, without conceiving of it as its own, without conceiving any relationship whatever.' (*Obras completas de Andrés Bello*, vol. III (Caracas), p. 145 n.)

57. 'The freedom of the prime cause is original and unlimited; the freedom of the human spirit is derived and finite; it is a faculty imprinted on man, like all the other faculties which his soul and body enjoy.' (ibid., p. 156.)

58. 'The Eternal Being is present at all moments of the duration of his works; for the Divinity there is no past or future, as there are for created intelligences' (ibid., p. 151).

59. 'There is for man a future destiny capable of satisfying his aspirations. The human soul survives death.' 'Divine beneficence and justice assure us that moral order receives its complement and perfection beyond the grave.' (ibid., pp. 166, 167.) We should note that, with respect to immortality, although he upholds the idea that 'reason alone is enough to see in the moral phenomena of which we are witnesses a future which awaits us after the grave', he also states that 'from what is immaterial and simple, the immortal does not necessarily follow'. (ibid., pp. 221, 220.)

60. 'The self which feels, perceives, remembers, imagines, judges, reasons, desires and wishes is to our conscience the same self, the same being, the same substance.' (ibid., p. 215.)

61. ibid., pp. 27ff., 339, 345, 253, 407–8.

62. ibid., pp. 416, 209, 682.

63. ibid., pp. 22–3.

64. ibid., p. 215.

65. ibid., p. 275.

66. Idea is the same as image or renewed perception; to conceive and to perceive is not 'always' exactly one and the same thing, etc. For examples see ibid., pp. 12, 25–6, 73–4.

67. ibid., pp. 256ff.

68. See the whole chapter 'Of the Intelligence of Animals', ibid., pp. 220–4.

69. ibid., p. 221.

70. ibid., p. 408. Thus, 'in order to think about two parallel lines in general, it is enough for me to imagine two parallel lines in a certain place, and of a certain length, colour, etc. and to think about mountains it is enough for me to imagine one or two, of certain size, shape and colours, at a certain distance at which the eye can easily take in their dimensions'. (ibid., p. 250.)

71. 'From the illusion that the use of abstract nouns produces have stemmed not a few of the absurdities which have contaminated for centuries the philosophy of understanding, and of which perhaps it has not been completely purged by the works of Locke, Berkeley, Condillac and other eminent philosophers. Hence the substantial forms of the peripatetic school, qualities to which were attributed a certain kind of independent reality. Hence so many erroneous concepts relative to space and time.' (ibid., p. 269; see also p. 187.)

72. ibid., pp. 124, 129, etc.

73. ibid., p. 380.

74. ibid., p. 219.

75. The quotations in this paragraph come from ibid., pp. 25, 367, 374, 640, 645.

76. ibid., p. 164.

77. ibid., p. 166.

78. ibid., p. 165.

79. *Obras completas de Andrés Bello*, vol. VIII (Santiago), p. 304: speech on his installation as Rector of the University.

2 The Poet

In his early adolescence Andrés Bello began to write poetry, and this should not surprise us, since that is the age when we all rough out a sonnet or two. But what was exceptional in him was the high quality which showed through in his early verses. In colonial Caracas, the fruit of a ripening cultural process, the mirror of a drive towards nationhood which culminated in the first decade of the nineteenth century, Bello was thought of as the poet *par excellence*, the man who was essential to enliven great occasions. In the intense life of salons and literary groups, somewhat reminiscent of the *philosophe* circles which led up to the French Revolution, with their basis of classical learning, there was a vogue for 'modern' literature which sharpened his poetical sensibility and provided a favourable *milieu* for his transitional poetry, moulding his admirable balance between romanticism and classicism.

Before he left Caracas he was justly famed as a good local poet. Some of his poems, such as his 'Ode to Vaccination' (written to commemorate the arrival of the expedition of Balmis, which brought smallpox vaccination to Venezuela), seem over-long with their boring tone of praise. In this poem, as in his ode 'Al Anauco', we find him tedious in his overburden of mythology and his typically neoclassical parade of the names of the ancients. But in his Virgilian eclogue 'Thirsis, who dwellst in shaded Tagus', we feel the presence of a tempered character, with an admirable command of the language, which flows like some gently bucolic melody. Bello's poetical nature is revealed also in his lyric 'A la nave', a Horatian imitation, and in his magnificent, though bombastic, sonnet on the victory of Bailén: 'The lion, in his pride, bursts the chains the villain thought must bind him', the turgidity of which is in complete contrast with the rest of his poetry.[1]

THE ARTISTIC LIBERATOR OF AMERICA

Bello the poet reached his peak in London. Deep study, which refined even more his command of language, the pains of exile, poverty, calumny and family troubles, all of which moulded his sensibility, and his heart-felt ambition to serve his country in the fields of letters since he was not able to take part with his contemporaries in the epic struggles for political freedom, combined to make him the 'artistic liberator of America', as Professor Edoardo Crema has said.[2] Don Arístides Rojas, one of the most devoted *bellistas*, had already declared:

From that day [when he wrote the *Silva a la agricultura de la zona tórrida*] Bello's genius is not the property of one nation, but belongs to the race which discovered America, founded a civilisation there, and imbued its daughter nations with love of glory, devotion to beauty and family feeling. . . . Before Bello, Spanish America meant literary obscurantism, art forced into a framework, the uninspired phrase, mute nature. Bello brought ideas, aesthetics, form, advance in use of language, the inspiration of an America full of splendid and prodigal nature, spontaneous as her rivers, rich as her seams of precious metals, magnificent as the Andes.[3]

Bello's *Silva a la agricultura de la zona tórrida* is the high-point of his poetry, but it was not the only important poem. His *Alocución a la poesía*, of the same period and inspired by the same ideas, must be given a place alongside from the point of view of Spanish American interest. But his *Moisés salvado de la aguas* or the *Canto al 18 de septiembre* (1841) reach the same artistic heights; and his *Oración por todos*, familiar in all the homes of Spanish America, a copy more famous than the original, firmly establishes his credentials as a poet.

As a poet Bello was classical and romantic at one and the same time. He was classical by education and by his direct knowledge of the great figures of ancient literature, by his defence of all things that in the best literary tradition brought no bar to the originality of the poet and the flight of imagination. But he was also a romantic because he followed the justified romantic criticism of the devotion to outmoded stereotyped forms and the imitativeness which reduced everything to the ploughing of the same furrow. He was an imitator at times, and many of his most inspired verses are like translations or copies of Hugo, Virgil or

Horace: but even in these he left his own clear mark. Perhaps he was thinking of this when he wrote: 'I have always thought that it was unjust to criticise and deny the accolade of creative genius to an author who treats new themes, whether or not in their rough state they possess the grandeur and beauty which alone give the palm of immortality to artistic works, and clothe them with forms which are new, beautiful, characteristic and interesting.'[4]

It is his poetry which has brought Bello the highest praise. I myself would not deny that his poems frequently savour of hard methodical work rather than of the inspiration of genius, but nevertheless inspiration abounds in his most famous work. Authorities have rightly pointed out that 'as a poet he combined the classical school with the romantic',[5] and that, as Manuel Cañete has said, he possessed 'the gift of success, in classical as well as in romantic productions'.[6] His poetry won the highest opinions of Menéndez y Pelayo and Miguel Antonio Caro. Cañete saw in it 'so much energy and greatness, so much variety and smoothness, such elevated philosophical thought, such polished and expressive versification, and such wealth of learned and picturesque expression' that in his Prologue to the works of another Spanish American poet, he gives Bello's verse the highest place in the reasons for his love and admiration of America.[7] One of the characteristics of Bello's poetry, stemming from his upbringing in the tropics, is his love of Nature. He never forgot his Nature, the Nature of the tropics, the Nature of Venezuela, which spoke to him in his rough drafts of the *Silva a la agricultura*: 'But no land cedes to yours, Venezuela, the joy of Nature if not of your spoiled people.'[8] This tropical nature must, in his memory, have seemed all the more beautiful in contrast with the land in which he was forced to spend his days. But nature, even in the exuberance of his *Silva a la agricultura*, is never just a subject for him, but is always an object regarded as an essential ingredient of human well-being. For another aspect of Bello is the teleological meaning of his poetry. He was no supporter of art for art's sake. He never wrote just for the sake of writing. Nearly all of Bello's poems were written with the same object in mind: that poetry is the vehicle for the diffusion of thought. The thought might include an important social idea, as in the *Silva*, which suggests a return to the land, which as time passes becomes a more urgent need,[9] praise of a man's merit, or a few words of sympathy. Francisco Vargas Fontecilla, Dean of the faculty of humanities of the University of Chile, said these words on the first centenary of Bello's birth: 'His grand verse served nothing but the healthiest morality and the purest sentiments.'[10] Bello's moral tone as a poet is pre-eminent in his best work, as Menéndez y Pelayo remarks, in comparing him 'with the patriarchs of the primitive peoples. . . . Philosophers and poets, who drew men to them with their verses, and then encouraged them to live together in society.' This was Bello's deliberate stance, as his verses testify in the last stanza of his poem *La moda*: 'Although in my verse no spark shines of that divine fire which kindles genius, and no rich eloquence adorns it, and in it all is lacking which could gratify men's taste, at least it is composed by a good and benign soul who is content with simplicity and truth.'[11]

A TREASURY OF AESTHETIC IDEAS

This attitude towards poetry had a firm basis in the treasury of Bello's aesthetic ideas. He was certainly a poet in the actual composition of such splendid poetical works, and he was also a poet in his approach in theory. This is no surprise in a philosopher, for whom every conscious act of man has its source in philosophy. A clear idea of 'the beautiful' and a logical construction of the means of attaining it, 'art', were the foundation of his literary activity.

The cornerstone of his literary theory is 'the innate sense of beauty which is in every man'.[12] This aesthetic feeling natural in man is absolute in that 'every new facet revealed to him in the ideal model of beauty thrills the human heart, created to admire and feel it';[13] but it is also relative, in that aesthetic taste appears 'in forms which are peculiar to each country and century'.[14]

Art serves to obtain beauty. As a means, it must fulfil the conditions demanded by the end sought. If the latter, beauty, has an absolute basis since it rests on human nature, but builds upon it constructions conditioned by the time and place, art must still respect 'the laws which cannot be denied, dictated by nature',[15] but should evolve with time and place to accompany the aesthetic sense in its evolution.

Bello shows himself here, as in his philosophy, as a classic, but a man of a tempered classicism reminiscent of the balance of the great classics. Accepting the influence of his time, convinced that romanticism, despite its excesses, was a healthy reaction against the pseudo-classicism which attempted to bind the mind to nothing more than servile and perpetual imitation of the ancient writers, he rejected 'the authority of those conventional laws which have been revived in order to force the mind to travel for ever along the railways of Greek and Latin poetry'.[16]

AN ADMIRABLE BALANCE

This admirable balance once again throws Bello's splendid mind into relief. He is above the academic sectarianism of his age, as he is in philosophy and grammar, and perceives what is common ground, and what is right, in the most opposed of human opinions.

His defence of the perennial teaching in the works of the classical authors is often repeated in his own writings. For example, when he speaks of Aristotle, praising his *Rhetoric* and his *Poetics* in the *Historia de la literatura*, Bello says: 'Aristotle, faithful interpreter of nature and reason, proclaims rules which are almost always wise and will be respected for ever, despite the attacks of bad taste against these healthy barriers, beyond which there is nothing but exaggeration and disagreement.'[17] Or, freely commenting on Cicero: 'We should not seek here [*De oratore*] profound aesthetic ideas, because the ancients never found them; instead they propounded general precepts applicable to all periods of literature, and which have never been better expressed.'[18] And so Bello, the object of constant attacks from the passionate supporters of extreme ideas, feels able to say: 'Only someone entirely unversed in the literary topics of our time could credit us with such an absurd idea as that of doing away with all rules, without exception, as if poetry were not an art, and there could be art without rules.'[19] 'The choice of new subjects and freedom of form, recognising only the unavoidable laws of intelligence and the noble instincts of the human heart, is what constitutes real poetry in every age and every land.'[20] Bello states that in poetry, as in every other literary *genre*, 'taste varies from one period to another, without surpassing the boundaries of what is legitimate and reasonable', and so 'in the theatre more than in any other artistic medium, variety is essential to capture attention'.[21] But Bello only means his gospel of liberty to extend to 'what is legitimate and reasonable'. Thus he condemned 'literary vandalism'[22] and made his most all-inclusive artistic profession of faith on the occasion – which could not have been more solemn – of his installation as Rector of the University of Chile. His words were:

'THIS IS MY LITERARY CREED'

At the same time the university will remind our young men of the advice of one of the great men of our time: 'Art must be the discipline of imagination', as Goethe has said, 'and must turn imagination into poetry.' Art! Some, when they hear that word, although taken from the lips of Goethe, will place me among the supporters of the conventional rules which usurped that name for a long time. I make the most solemn protest against any such assertion; and I do not believe that anything I have done justifies it. I do not find art in the sterile precepts of some school, in the inexorable unities, in the wall of bronze dividing the different styles and *genres*, or in the chains in which poets have been bound in the name of Aristotle and Horace, attributing to these, at times, ideas which they never had. But I believe that there does exist an art based on the impalpable, ethereal relations of ideal beauty; relations which are delicate, but visible to the keen eye of a competently trained mind; I believe that there is an art which guides the imagination in its most spirited flights; I believe that without that art, the fancy, instead of embodying in its creation the model of beauty, brings forth mis-shapen hybrids, unformed and monstrous offspring. This is my literary creed. Liberty in everything – but I do not see liberty, but rather licentious intoxication, in orgies of the imagination.[23]

Bello's strong feeling that literature was the 'Corinthian capital' as it were, of cultivated society[24] led him to attack 'the extravagances of that so-called literary liberty which, under pretext of throwing off the yoke of Aristotle and Horace, respects neither language nor common sense, at times even breaks the rules of decency, insults religion and thinks it has discovered a new kind of sublimity in blasphemy'.[25] He sees romanticism, however, not as the negation of art but as its transformation:

Thus, a large part of the precepts of Aristotle and Horace is as precisely observed by the romantic school as by the classical; and it must be so, because these precepts are versions and corollaries of the principle of the fidelity of imitation, and are essential means of pleasing. But there are other rules which critics who favour the classical school regard as obligatory, but which those who favour the romantic school deem useless or even pernicious. Among these rules are the three unities, and especially the unities of place and time.[26]

Innovation in art is essential to fit it to 'the circumstances of each epoch' and to give art 'original features: thus Shakespeare and Calderón enlarged the compass of the spirit and showed that all art was not contained in the works of Sophocles or Molière, or in the precepts of Aristotle or Boileau'.[27]

'Romanticism, in this sense, does not recognise the classifications of ancient art,' but it assumes recognition of the basic laws of all aesthetic production: 'the condition that art should be hidden does not mean it must be proscribed. There must be art.'[28] Live, dynamic, spontaneous art, like that of the 'ancient Castilian poets (if we may be allowed to call such those who flourished in the sixteenth and seventeenth centuries)', such as 'Quevedo, Lope, Calderón, Góngora, and even Garcilaso, Rioja and Herrera', in whom he sees 'fluency, passion, fecundity, vigour, frequently irregular and even uncontrolled, but who even in their exaggerations bear the stamp of greatness and daring which imposes respect'.[29] On the other hand he was not in sympathy with those poets who from the sixteenth century 'abandoned the simple and expressive naturalism of the older poetry' and adopted a style which was 'too artificial', and which 'entirely because of its elegance and flights of fancy lost a great deal of the old facility and fluency and was rarely successful in translating the emotions of the soul with vigour and purity'.[30] For these reasons he criticises poets such as Luzán ('correct, but without vigour') and Meléndez (who 'have a rich, choice, lively style yet with an air of study and effort, and with some taint of affectation') and also even Jovellanes and Cienfuegos, in whom he decries their archaicisms and, naturally, 'the cosmetics of modern Gongorism'; whilst at the same time he praises Lope, the Argensolas and Rioja, in his critique of Heredia.[31]

Classic and romantic as Bello was, both in his aesthetic ideas and in his own poetry, he regarded the primacy of laws over art as essential, meanwhile maintaining his faithfulness to classical principles and condemning the excesses of the romantic school. If morality rules human conduct and art is made by man, then art cannot be an exception in the behaviour of a free and rational being. 'Impiety and sensuality can be a lure for some readers; but a naturally noble soul, one exceptionally well endowed, must disdain to use them.'[32] 'Even in its daring, poetry must respect certain limits and only infrequently lose sight of truth and, in particular, justice.'[33] Truth, good and beauty are an inseparable trilogy in Bello's thought and work.[34]

The aesthetic ideas which were inseparable from Bello's poetical efforts also accompanied him in his valuable and prolific critical work.

THE CRITIC

The excerpts we have quoted testify to Bello's stern yet generous critical work. In his didactic writings, his newspaper articles and his various essays his intention was to give a lead with respect to the ancient and modern values which appeared most acceptable on account of their merit or their popularity. He observed no taboo on the ancients when he pointed out their errors but neither did he disdain to applaud and encourage the moderns.

A part of this critical work springs from Bello's scholarly love of literary research, carried out more for pleasure and mental exercise than for teaching and wide publication. Here, for example, belong Bello's valuable researches into the *Poema de Mío Cid*, the fruit of many years of thought and analysis, a jewel of criticism in Castilian, which drew from Menéndez y Pelayo the remark: 'Bello's work, carried out almost entirely by his own individual efforts is even now, taken as a whole, the most thorough that we have on the *Poema de Mío Cid*.'[35] The other part of Bello's critical work belongs more to the teacher together with the journalist acting as a benign director of opinion. He knew that the cultural life of any society needs a good critic, of sound education and unbiased views, capable of seizing the full meaning of a work and weighing its importance. He should be warm-hearted enough to encourage new young writers but not hesitate to point out errors and defects. In sum, he must be a critic who does not indulge in systematic disparagement or exaggerated praise, with sufficient ability and authority to express his honest opinion firmly but not cruelly, with kindness but without flattery. In default of someone else who would take on this role, and despite his numerous commitments, Bello became this critic for Chile.

In his *Literatura* and from the columns of journals Bello formed the opinions of his school of followers about the figures of ancient literature and the publicists of his time. He points out defects in Homer, Virgil, Ovid and Horace, just as he does in the great names of his day,[36] and if at times he falls into critical trivialities, he does it especially in dealing with the demanding sticklers for the rules, as in his judgement of Hermosilla,[37] or when he maintains a long and fruitless polemic with José Joaquín de Mora.[38] His view of literary authorities is brilliantly condensed in a paragraph about the Spanish Academy:

We count ourselves among those who most appreciate the work of the Spanish Academy, but we are not among those who regard its decisions with a sort of superstitious veneration, as if it were not, like Homer, able to nod from time to time, or as if it possessed some sort of sovereignty over the language to order it to be spoken and written in a manner other than that demanded by good usage or advised by plain reason.[39]

And so Bello, as he told the University of Chile, took care to welcome in practice 'liberty, as opposed on the one hand to the docile servility which accepts everything without examination, and on the other to the disorderly licence which rebels against the rule of reason and against the noblest and purest instincts of the human heart'.[40]

Bello's work in Chile would have been incomplete without his enormous work of criticism. Through it he tried to purify literary taste, historical opinion and social outlook. He fought for simplicity in the use of Spanish, as when he criticised the classicists' 'mania for replacing a proper noun by a poetical definition of the object';[41] he sought moral and social utility in literature, expressing his desire that 'there should be more productions based on domestic and innocent emotions, and less of the erotic kind, of which in our language we already have a pernicious superfluity'.[42] Bello also concerned himself with the theatre, and in *El araucano* defended it as a means of education and amusement. He was a great play-goer, and did not keep his impressions to himself. He gave out his opinions in the press, keeping the public informed and stimulated by his own ideas. Of course, his reviews were more concerned with the plays than with the acting. He condemned immorality in the theatre, and tried to popularise recitation both as an art in itself and as a means of purifying the language of the people.[43] When we read and think over Bello's constant and warm-hearted critical work, we feel all the more the lack in many of the literary fields of Spanish America of critics such as he, with the combination of masterly authority, patriotic generosity and honest uprightness of opinion.

CHAPTER 2: NOTES AND REFERENCES

1. Pedro Grases has shown that Bello's poetical production in Caracas includes the play *España restaurada, o El certamen de los patriotas*, presented in the Caracas Coliseum in December 1808. See Pedro Grases, *La singular historia de un drama y un soneto de Andrés Bello* (Caracas: 1943).

2. *El drama artístico de Andrés Bello*, unpublished as a book, but some of whose chapters, including 'Tras del Libertador político, el Libertador artístico', have been presented in lectures and periodicals. See *Revista nacional de cultura*, nos 19, 23, 24 (June–December 1942).

3. Arístides Rojas, 'Infancia y juventud de Bello', and 'Cuna y tumba', in *Estudios históricos*, 2nd series (Caracas: 1927), pp. 33 and 108.

4. *Obras completas de Andrés Bello*, vol. IX (Caracas), p. 366.

5. Zorrilla de San Martin, *Compendio de la historia de la literatura*, p. 613.

6. Quoted in Amunátegui, op. cit., p. 594.

7. Quoted by Arístides Rojas, 'Infancia y juventud de Bello', pp. 33–4 (in his Introduction to the poetry of the Cuban Mendive).

8. *Obras completas de Andrés Bello*, vol. II (Caracas), p. 55. The published text speaks of 'Thine own fertile soil'. See also Prologue by Barnola, pp. xlivff, 'La presencia de Venezuela'.

9. 'Oh young nations, whose brow is crowned with laurel, to the astonishment of the older east! Honour the land, the simple life of the ploughman, and his simple ways.' (*Obras completas de Andrés Bello*, vol. I (Caracas), p. 74.)

10. *Obras completas de Andrés Bello*, vol. IV (Santiaogo), pp. xi–xii.

11. *Obras completas de Andrés Bello*, vol. I (Caracas), p. 276.

12. ibid., vol. IX, p. 451: 'Juicio sobre los ensayos literarios y críticos de Alberto Lista'.

13. *Obras completas de Andrés Bello*, vol. VIII (Santiago), p. 307; Bello's speech at his installation as Rector of the University of Chile.

14. ibid., vol. VI, p. 281: 'Observaciones sobre la "Historia de la literatura española" de Jorge Ticknor'.

15. *Obras completas de Andrés Bello*, vol. IX (Caracas), p. 452: 'Juicio sobre los ensayos . . . de Alberto Lista'.

1. Plaza Bolivar, Caracas, in the early 19th Century

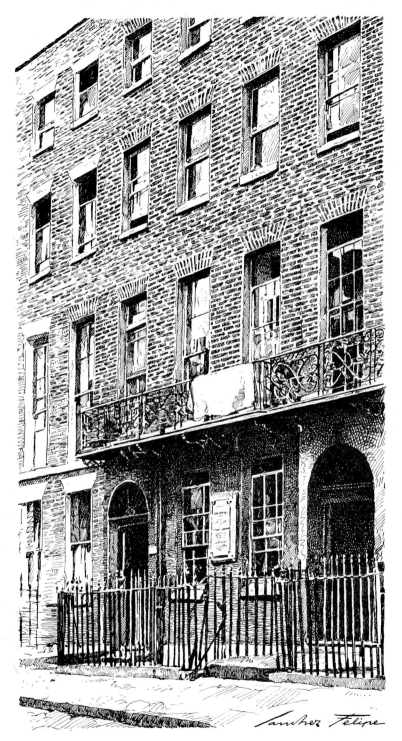

3. 58 Grafton Way, the London home of Francisco de Miranda

4. Bust of Andrés Bello by August François. Erected in 1882 at the University of Chile, Santiago

16. ibid., p. 359: 'Juicio sobre *La araucana* de Ercilla'.

17. ibid., p. 73.

18. ibid., p. 184.

19. ibid., p. 705.

20. ibid., p. 459: 'Juicio sobre los ensayos . . .' de Alberto Lista.

21. ibid., p. 708: 'Teatro'.

22. ibid., Vol. VIII, p. 491.

23. *Obras completas de Andrés Bello*, vol. VIII (Santiago), p. 317.

24. ibid., p. 316.

25. *Obras completas de Andrés Bello*, vol. IX (Caracas), p. 449. He put this condemnation of exaggerated romanticism into verse in his *La moda*, in which, in the guise of advice from this goddess to a poet, he ridiculed the outrages of the literary extremism at that time 'modern'. Here is an example: 'Virtue now? There is no room for that in this century of light and progress. Let the mad din stun with infernal hullabaloo where grim Timon, half seas over, jeers and taunts. Let swords gleam among the cups; let there be killing and rowdy laughter; and in Satanic songs let bold blasphemy boom, dreadful, outrageous, but delicious sauce to educated palates.' (O.C. Caracas I, p. 275).

26. ibid., p. 705: 'Teatro'.

27. ibid., p. 452: 'Juicio sobre los ensayos . . .' de Alberto Lista.

28. ibid., p. 451.

29. ibid., p. 199: 'Juicio sobre Cienfuegos'.

30. ibid., p. 361: 'Juicio sobre *La araucana* de Ercilla'. Bello defends Ercilla against the sticklers for the rules: 'But Ercilla's moderate and familiar tone, which, we must confess, at times degenerates into dullness and triviality, could scarcely avoid diminishing the merit of his poem in the eyes of the Spaniards of that age of refined elegance and grandiose pomposity which succeeded to the more healthy and pure taste of poets such as Garcilaso and Luis de León.'

31. ibid., p. 243.

32. *Obras completas de Andrés Bello*, vol VIII (Santiago), p. 424: memorandum to the university in 1854

33. *Obras completas de Andrés Bello*, vol IX (Caracas), p. 250: Critique of *El triunfo de Ituzaingó* by Juan Cruz Varela, from *Repertorio americano* (1827).

34. His judgement that it is defective art to be obscene is made clear in his *Historia de la literatura*, where he condemns 'the shocking obscenity of language' in Catullus, almost at the level of Aristophanes; criticises Propertius for 'having more than once overstepped the bounds of decency; and even condemns some of the odes of Horace for their indecency. (ibid., pp. 135–6, 138, 167.)

35. On this subject see Pedro Grases, *La épica española y los estudios de Andrés Bello sobre el 'Poema del Cid'* (Caracas: 1954). Bello's writings on the Cid will appear in *Obras completas de Andrés Bello*, vol. VII (Caracas), with Prologue by Pedro Grases.

36. *Obras completas de Andrés Bello*, vol. IX (Caracas), pp 43, 146, 152, 153, 167: *Historia de la literatura*.

37. ibid., pp. 373ff.

38. Amunátegui, op. cit., pp. 326–38.
39. *Obras completas de Andrés Bello*, vol. V (Caracas), p. 119: 'Diccionario de la lengua castellana por la Academia Española'.
40. *Obras completas de Andrés Bello*, vol. VIII (Santiago), p. 317: 'Discurso de instalación de la Universidad'.
41. *Obras completas de Andrés Bello*, vol. IX (Caracas), p. 378: Critique of José Gómez Hermosilla.
42. ibid., p. 242: 'Juicio sobre Heredia'.
43. Amunátegai, op. cit., pp. 437–51.

3 *The Philologist*

One of the titles which can least be denied to Bello is that of philologist, in the widest sense of the word. He made a thorough study of all branches of learning connected with language; and if it is true that, in general, he only wrote about them as a teacher, we can still deduce from his various writings the complete framework of his philological ideas. He began by applying philosophy to language; he gained a practical knowledge of Greek, Latin, Spanish, French, English and Italian, and tried to go back to their historical origins and evolution; and in literature he found a wide field for his philological research, and gave loving attention to grammar, the study of which he defended staunchly.

Philosophy which, in the classical manner, was the basis of all Bello's speculations, was also the foundation of his philological studies.[1] He wrote:

There are few things that give the mind exercise more apt to develop its faculties and make them agile and nimble than the philosophical study of language. It has been believed, without any foundation, that learning a language is exclusively the work of memory. No sentence can be constructed, no good translation can be made from one language into another, without a scrutiny of the most intimate relationships of ideas, without an examination under a microscope, so to say, of their accidence and modifications. This branch of study is not so bereft of attractions as those who have not gained some familiarity with it think. In the subtle and fleeting analogies on which the choice of forms of verbs depends (and the same could be said of some other parts of language) we find a marvellous inter-linking of metaphysical relationships, bound together with an order and precision which are surprising when we consider that they are entirely due to popular usage, the true and only maker of languages. The meanings of verbal inflections seem at first to be a chaos in which everything is arbitrary, irregular and capricious; but in the light of analysis this apparent disorder becomes clear, and in its place we see a system of general laws which work with absolute uniformity and which are even capable of being expressed in strict formulae, which can be built up and broken down just as can those of the language of the algebra.[2]

THE LIVING INSTRUMENT OF SOCIAL COHESION

In Bello's comprehensive view of language we see the dominance of that marvellous synthesis of tradition and innovation which characterises all his work. In his defence of tradition he was 'the saviour of the integrity of Castilian in Spanish America'.[3] To safeguard this integrity he recommended to the university the study of 'the classics of our language, which are regarded too disdainfully, especially when they are studied and admired more than ever by the most cultivated nations of Europe'.[4] And because of this he was nicknamed 'the purist', in the pejorative sense of the word. But in fact he was a grammatical revolutionary, since he realised that 'languages are like organised bodies which constantly assimilate new elements, taking them from the society in which they live, and adapting them under the form appropriate to each language to the ideas which are dominant in each society: ideas which are being incessantly renewed by external motives, like the atmosphere which vegetables feed on'.[5] The problem of the origin of language occupies Bello's attention in a chapter of his *Filosofía del entendimiento*,[6] where he makes an exposition of this subject, using Reid's ideas as a guide.

Bello's philological philosophy starts from the proposition that in philology, as in other branches of learning, there are certain general principles derived from human nature, on which is built a structure which varies according to historical circumstances.

There is no doubt that the symbols of thought obey certain general laws which, derived from those to which thought itself is subject, rule all languages and form a universal grammar. But if we except the conversion of reasoning into propositions and of the proposition into subject and attribute; the existence of the noun to express directly objects, that of the verb to indicate attributes, and that of other words which modify and determine nouns and verbs, in order that, with a limited number of these, all possible objects can be designated, not only real but also intellectual ones, and all attributes we perceive in objects; if we except this basic framework of languages, then I see nothing that we are obliged to recognise as a universal law from which no language can be exempt.[7]

Consequently Bello firmly rejected the etymological tendency which attempts to direct language by the rules of past phases which are historical categories, now out of date. To find grammatical correctness, the source which should be studied above all is 'popular usage, the true and only maker of languages'.[8] In the Prologue to his *Gramática de la lengua castellana*, Bello writes: 'I would reduce the philosophy of grammar to the representation of usage under the simplest and most comprehensive formulae.'[9]

And therefore Bello also condemned the strict tendency which seeks to keep a language static, as if we were still in the sixteenth century. 'We should be very sparing in admitting neologisms, especially in Spanish America, where a linguistic orgy would lead to the breaking-up of the language, as Latin broke up into the romance languages, and thus we should lose the precious wealth which Castile bestowed on our continent. But neither should we forbid the entry of new words which answer new concepts or express them better than other words already established by prior use.' This was what Bello taught, and he repeated his views many times. Here are some examples:

We are not purists; we do not claim that we should resort to Cervantes or Fray Luis de Granada for the words needed to translate into our language the ideas of Laromiguière, Kant or Cousin. But we believe that, with the exception of a small number of technical nouns whose meaning has been fixed by acceptable definitions deduced from the generation of these ideas, our language does not lack the means to express the most abstract thoughts, and to depict them with grace.[10]

I shall never advocate that exaggerated purism which condemns everything new in the field of language. On the contrary, I believe that the flood of new ideas which pass daily from literary use to general circulation demands new words to describe them. . . . But language can be widened, enriched and accommodated to the demands of fashion, which holds undeniable sway over literature, without adulterating it, or corrupting its constructions, or doing violence to its spirit.[11]

Incorrect grammar and the abuse of neologisms tarnish all branches of our literature: in the law courts, in academic lectures, in political discussions, in clerical oratory. Outside a few well-known exceptions, everything that comes off our presses bears this ugly stamp. I say the abuse of neologisms, because I am not inclined to praise that mean purism which seeks to stereotype languages and which, when everything is progressing, and original ideas and great creations abound on all sides, stubbornly tries to clothe them in the garb of other centuries, which never even guessed at them from afar. This is like the painter in the story who, to compete with Velazquez, dressed the contemporaries he portrayed in the garments of the Court of Philip II.[12]

When he reviewed Heredia, Bello criticised, as he had in Cienfuegos, the abuse of archaicisms, caused by 'the contagion of bad example',[13] and in his review of Hermosilla he quoted Horace in defence of the introduction of new words which represented new ideas.[14]

Although the meaning of the sentences quoted is not merely clear, but even diaphanous, we should look carefully at what they say. 'I am not a purist', Bello says, insofar as purist means one who writes or speaks with exaggerated affectation in the desire to do so with excessive correctness; although he was indeed a strict purist in the sense of one who writes or speaks with correctness and cares about the purity of the language. Bello's concern was that language should serve its social aims; and thus it was that he urged so strongly the need for 'clarity, the most essential virtue of language, which through a misfortune of Castilian has been the most neglected one in all periods of its literature'.[15]

Once we have explained Bello's position as regards neologisms, we need hardly go on to say that he defended the freedom of new metaphorical usages of already established words; for if he supported the freedom to introduce new words, how could he reject freedom for new meanings, not arbitrary, but simply analogous to those already accepted? The following sentences simply serve as a new manifestation of the harmony of Bello's teaching: 'It would be no small absurdity if words could not take metaphorical meanings other than those announced by the *Diccionario de la Real Academia.* . . .' 'Novelty of images is properly one of the qualities which enhance their legitimate use, even in the didactic style.'[16]

The many philological writings of Bello (here I am referring to those strictly about language, since many of the opinions I have quoted appear in works of very diverse natures) can be classified, excluding separate articles, according to four main themes: language and metre in poetry, spelling, conjugation, and Castillian and general grammar.

CORRECT LANGUAGE AND METRE IN POETRY

In 1835 Bello published in Santiago a book entitled *Principios de la ortología y métrica de la lengua castellana*, and by his death two other editions had been published (1850 and 1859), which testifies to the success of the book. His aim was to satisfy the need for the study of orthology for, as he said in the Prologue to the first edition,

it is not enough for the words to be fitting and the sentences correct if the legitimate sounds, quantities and accents are not used. This study is highly necessary to prevent the rapid degeneration which otherwise languages would suffer and which would bring about a multiplicity of languages, increasing the obstacles in the way of communication and human intercourse, which are such powerful means of increasing civilisation and prosperity. It is indispensable to those who by their place in society could not without humiliation reveal in their language the taint of vulgarity or ignorance. The omission of this study discredits the orator and can even make him ridiculous and incite the scorn of his hearers. And finally, it is a study which should be undertaken by all those who aspire to the cultivation of poetry, or at the least to enjoy in their reading of poetry those exquisite mental pleasures produced by the representation of physical and moral nature, and which contribute so much to the improvement and polishing of customs.[17]

In his book Andrés Bello planned to keep off the well-worn track of those whose intention was to make Castilian orthography a mere appendage of etymology or simply the product of abstract speculations. General usage is the prime rule from which all Bello's secondary rules are derived; the ear is the basis of his rules of metre; and abundance of examples is his principal method of teaching.

He fought a long campaign to prove that the rhythm of the romance languages is fundamentally different from that of Greek and Latin. Rhythm, which 'in general is the division of time into equal parts, by means of similar sounds or pauses which end or indicate them', and which 'we could say is the symmetry of time, which is composed of successive elements, as the symmetry which we perceive in space consists of parts whose existence is simultaneous',[18] this rhythm in the ancient languages is based on quantity, whereas in the romance languages it springs from accentuation. Theorists who wanted to emphasise the similarity between the modern languages and their sources asserted the contrary, but the patient and unremitting struggle ended in victory for the Venezuelan scholar's thesis.

Bello's metre is classical, and perhaps today may appear strict. But he was not a partisan of rhyme: 'accents and pauses', he said, 'are absolutely essential, but sometimes there is no need for rhyme'.[19] Bello's section on elision and hiatus gained special praise from Menéndez y Pelayo. In sum it can be said that this is one of the basic works in Spanish grammar. Its greatest accolade, because of the authority from which it came, was given by the Spanish Academy, which wrote to him (27 June 1852):

The Commission appointed by this Academy to draw up a treatise on the prosody of the Castilian language, has made its report. In this it declares that, having examined all the works published up to the present on this important subject, it judges that there is nothing or almost nothing new to be done; and considering, after a careful scrutiny, that this task has been fulfilled satisfactorily in your book, it is of the opinion that the Academy should adopt it providing you give your consent, and reserving to itself the right, if it judges it opportune, to make notes and corrections, since its opinions do not exactly coincide with yours. But recognising your right of property, in a meeting on the 25th of the present month, the Academy, after approval of the said report, agreed that you should be asked for your permission for it to be published under the terms indicated by the said Commission.[20]

REFORM OF SPANISH SPELLING

But if Bello's ideas on prosody met not only acceptance in theory but also practical application in language, the spelling reforms which he proposed remain in the world of the desirable, and with a few exceptions have had no practical effect.

Bello's campaign for the reform of Spanish spelling began with the article 'Indicaciones sobre la conveniencia de simplificar y uniformar la ortografía en América', which García del Río and he published in 1823 in the *Biblioteca americana*. The faculty of humanities of the University of Chile introduced similar modifications in 1844, and in defence of these innovations Bello wrote various articles, as before he had done in defence of the proposals in the *Biblioteca americana*. All these writings had the same general aim, which, with the object of simplifying the written language, counselled the immediate acceptance of a few reforms so that as the language progressed they should continue towards the goal of achieving complete correspondence between the written and the spoken language.

The basic rules of this evolution were:

1. To progress towards the perfection of the alphabet, which, as everyone knows, means that each simple sound should be represented by a single letter.
2. To suppress any letter which does not represent or contribute to the representation of a sound.
3. Not to give at present to any letter or combination of letters a value which it does not now usually have in the writing of the Spanish-speaking countries.
4. Not to introduce a large number of reforms at any one time.[21]

According to these rules, the *Biblioteca americana* delineated the course of future progress:

EPOCA PRIMERA –
1. To substitute *j* for *x* and *g* in all cases where the last two letters have the Arabic guttural sound.
2. To substitute *i* for *y* in all cases where the latter represents a simple vowel.
3. To suppress *h*.
4. To write with *rr* all syllables which contain the strong sound which corresponds to this letter.
5. To substitute *z* for soft *c*.
6. To banish the mute *u* accompanying *q*.
EPOCA SEGUNDA –
7. To substitute *q* for hard *c*.
8. To suppress the mute *u* which accompanies *g* in some words.[22]

The first and second innovations are used in the spelling of the Santiago edition of the *Obras completas de Andrés Bello*.[23] This system, put forward with no claim of originality,[24] and still regarded in some points as a simple consequence of the reforms advocated by the Spanish Academy,[25] is without doubt very well conceived from the theoretical point of view: it simplifies the art of writing, stops good spelling from being the possession of select groups, and is in complete correspondence with the essence of the spoken language. But nowadays would its usefulness compensate for the almost unimaginable task of smashing present usage? Would the benefit of scientific spelling captivate writers so that they would bear with a troublesome period of transition and undertake the reconstruction of the system of associations of images, which ensures that at the slightest impression which a written word produces on the optic nerve, the image of the spoken word immediately responds, and with it the idea which that word represents? This practical aspect has up to now been the obstacle which has prevented the adoption of Bello's system, in spite of the fact that all those who study it praise it. Usage, the prime rule of Bello's *Filología*, has proved stronger than his most powerful arguments, but there are hopeful signs leading to the possibility of reform. 'The desire for simplicity which has always kept Spanish spelling on the same lines as the living pronunciation is still latent there,' writes Angel Rosenblat in his Introduction to Bello's ideas on orthography: 'Simplicity of spelling has been a Hispanic ideal from Quintilian up to the present day. . . . The efforts of Don Andrés Bello to bring Spanish spelling closer to educated and general pronunciation obey one of most persistent tendencies of the Hispanic spirit. . . . A hundred years is a short time in the history of a language to make any prediction on the future of his ideas.'[26]

Bello also pleaded for the division of words into syllables to be made according to the pronunciation, following the general rule, in the case of an intermediate consonant, of attaching to the following vowel any consonant found at the beginning of a word, except for a few exceptions. The rules which he proposed in this respect have been accepted, and they have been extended to cases which the Venezuelan philologist, basing himself on the usage of his time, considered as exceptions.

IDEOLOGICAL ANALYSIS OF VERB CONJUGATION

Bello's *Análisis ideológica de los tiempos de la conjugación castellana* was in fact a product of colonial Venezuela, since it dates from before 1810,[27] and was published only in 1841. Such a long period explains the perfection and unity of the work. It is highly original, and even indispensable for the conscious and correct usage of the verbal forms of Spanish.

The names which Bello gives to the tenses: present, co-existence of the attribute with the moment of speaking; prete-rite, antecedence of the attribute to the act of the word; future, subsequence of the attribute to the act of the word; co-preterite, coexistence of the attribute with something past; post-preterite, subsequence of the attribute to something past; and ante-present, ante-preterite, ante-future, ante-co-preterite and ante-post-preterite: all these are undoubtedly more adequate to their 'primary meaning' than those still in use, and they make the study of grammar considerably easier, since in themselves they give an idea of the use and meaning of the tenses. This nomen-clature applied also to the moods of verbs, which Bello classifies as 'what the grammarians call' indicative, subjunctive, hypo-thetical subjunctive and optative, completed by an explanation of the secondary meanings of the indicative forms and by a trea-tise on the metaphorical meanings of verbal forms in general, constitutes a complete and harmonious system for the study of the Castilian verb.

The book is based on quotations from the best Spanish authors, some of whom he criticises at times. It has abundant illustrative notes referring to Latin, Greek and even modern languages, and thus he could say in the Prologue: 'This analysis of the tenses is limited in particular to the Castilian conjugation; but I am convinced that the procedure and principles which appear in Castilian are, with certain modifications, applicable to the other languages; and of these I have attempted to give examples in some of the notes which accompany the text.'[28] Bello's article 'De los tiempos latinos comparados con los cas-tellanos', published in the corrected edition he made of his son Francisco's Latin Grammar, is truly a complement of his *Análisis ideológica* for students of Latin who are well grounded in Castilian grammar.

Characteristic of the spirit of the centenary of Bello's death was the resolution of the Academies of Language of the Spanish-speaking countries recommending that in all these countries the teaching and nomenclature of the tenses should be carried out according to the Venezuelan scholar's system.[29]

A MONUMENT: THE GRAMMAR

The synthesis of all Bello's knowledge of grammar was his *Gramática de la lengua castellana destinada al uso de los americanos*, published in 1847. On 16 May of that year he announced the fact to his brother Carlos: 'During these days they are finishing the printing of a Castilian grammar which I have written, and in which you will find many new things.'[30] His theories on prosody and verbs were quickly re-echoed in this book, and are among the main innovations it contains; and the basic object of the work as a whole is the establishment of Castilian grammar as something independent of Latin grammar.

Andrés Bello was certainly a supporter of the study of Latin, but he was also an upholder of the complete difference between the grammars of Castilian and its mother-language. This was his principal undertaking; and his complete success is vouched for by Menéndez y Pelayo: 'To him we owe, more than to anyone else, the emancipation of our language's grammar from its servitude to Latin, which men have stupidly tried to adapt to an organism so diverse as that of the romance languages.'[31]

One of these remnants of Latin was brought to the fore by an attempt to assimilate the Castilian language to the system of declensions of the language of Latium, and it was one of those that Bello attacked with most calm, substituting for it a system more suitable for Castilian.[32]

That Bello intended his *Grammar* to be used for teaching was reflected even in the printing, done with two different types, one for the indispensable facts, and the other for the more or less full illustrative material. But its most interesting part is the notes which Bello added at the end; for these display, without limits imposed by the needs of teaching, his opinions which do not coincide with traditional grammar.

To help even more in the teaching of elementary grammar, Bello published a *Compendio de la gramática castellana escrito para el uso de las escuelas primarias*, whose first edition appeared in 1851, and the second, somewhat more developed, in 1861. This book is completely designed for teaching, with its large number of examples, special insistence on incorrect habits in general use and its absolutely practical system of definitions. 'In the definitions', he says in the Foreword, 'we have not attempted rigorous exactness. We have tried to point out objects, as with the finger, rather than try to explain them in precise formulas, which are rarely understood by the intelligence of children'.[33]

In his desire to make this subject easy, sure and objective, Bello at the time of his death was preparing a new book on it, intended for young students, to be called simply *Gramática castellana*. The discovery and publication of the manuscripts of this interesting work is due to the sympathetic research and excellent analysis of Miguel Luis Amunátegui.[34]

'FOR THE USE OF SPANISH AMERICANS'

Bello's *Grammar* was dedicated to the Spanish Americans, and its purpose was to preserve the purity of the language among them. When he explains his aim, he speaks again with eloquence about the question of neologisms, about new meanings of old words, and about false purity. But what he brings out most clearly is his idea of the need for unity – integration we should say today – among the Spanish American nations.

I do not claim to write for Castilians. My lessons are aimed at my brothers, the inhabitants of Spanish America. I believe it is important to preserve the language of our ancestors as pure as possible, as a providential means of communication and an instrument of fraternity between the various nations of Spanish origin spread over the two continents. But it is no superstitious purism that I dare to recommend. The astonishing advance in all the sciences and arts, the diffusion of intellectual culture, and political revolutions, every day require new signs to express new ideas; and the introduction of brand-new words, taken from the ancient and modern foreign languages, no longer offends us when it is not clearly unnecessary or when it does not reveal the affectation and bad taste of those who think that they are adorning in this way what they write. There is a worse vice: that of lending new meanings to words and phrases already in use, so multiplying the ambiguities from which, because of the variety of meanings of each word, more or less all languages suffer, and perhaps in greater proportion the more developed ones, through the almost infinite number of ideas to which it is necessary to fit a necessarily limited number of signs. But the greatest evil of all, and the one which, if it is not cut off, will deprive us of the inestimable advantages of a common language, is the entry of neologisms in constructions, which floods and confuses a large part of what is written in Spanish America, and by altering the structure of the language, tends to convert it into a multitude of irregular, anarchical, barbaric dialects, the embryos of future languages, which during a prolonged development would reproduce in Spanish America what there was in Europe in the dark period of the corruption of Latin. Chile, Peru, Buenos Aires, Mexico would each speak its own language, or rather, various languages, as is the case in Spain, Italy and France, where certain provincial languages are dominant, but various others live beside them and put obstacles in the way of the spread of learning, the execution of the laws, the administration of the state, and the unity of the nation. A language is like a living body: its vitality does not consist of the constant identity of elements, but of the regular uniformity with which the latter exercise their functions, and from which proceed the form and character which distinguish the whole.[35]

In his *Grammar*, as in his poetry, the vigorous personality of Bello appears as an expression of his authentic Spanish Americanism, transformed here into a luminous vision of the unity of the continent.

Andrés Bello's *Grammar* has received much well-deserved praise from all quarters.[36] I shall only mention the following opinions, which are all the more trustworthy because they come from Spain itself.

'This is perhaps the best *Grammar* of all those which have been written in recent times, including that of the Real Academia Española,' said Manuel Cañete in a session of that very Academy.[37]

It is 'without doubt the *Grammar* which has had the most reprintings in our century, has been studied by the greatest number of people, and has attracted the most famous commentators and apologists,' was the opinion of Menéndez y Pelayo;[38] though it is true that at the same time he recalled the names of Cuervo and Caro – to which that of Juan Vicente González might be added – whose editions 'have given new lustre to Bello's treatises on grammar'.

The Spanish Academy itself regarded Bello's work so highly

that it wrote to the Spanish Legation in Chile: 'The Royal Academy desires to give to this great scholar some public recognition of its opinion of his writings, and so it has appointed him an honorary Academician. This is the first time that this distinction has been granted since the publication of the new regulations,' and at the same time it sent the diploma, signed by Francisco Martínez de la Rosa and Juan Nicasio Gallego. 'Some years later, when the class of Corresponding Academicians was created, the Academy accepted the proposal of Don Manuel Cañete, of the 28 February 1861, to include Bello as a member of this new class.'[39] Although this *Grammar* was, modestly, intended for the Spanish Americans, it excited the interest of the specialists in the mother country. No clearer opinion could be found than that of Amado Alonso in his Introduction to Bello's grammatical studies in the Caracas edition of the *Obras completas*:

La gramática de la lengua castellana, written by Andrés Bello over a century ago, is still the best Spanish *Grammar* we have. . . . I know of no *Grammar* which could emerge so successfully from the rigorous examination to which we are submitting this one. It is a *Grammar* which attempted to be educative and not speculative, composed over a hundred years ago, precisely in the century in which the study of language became a science. We are examining it from a strictly linguistic point of view, not simply comparing it with the most accepted *Grammars*, and even so it still stands as a living contribution, not merely as the best Spanish *Grammar* because there is none better, but as one of the best *Grammars* of modern times in any language.[40]

CHAPTER 3: NOTES AND REFERENCES

1. See the assertion of García Bacca in the Prologue to Bello's *Filosofía*, *Obras completas de Andrés Bello*, vol. III (Caracas), p. xiv.
2. ibid., vol. V, pp. 6–7: 'Analísis ideológica'.
3. Menéndez y Pelayo, op. cit., p. cxxviii.
4. *Obras completas de Andrés Bello*, vol. VIII (Santiago), p. 377. Speech on the anniversary of the foundation of the university, 1848. In *Obras completas de Andrés Bello* (Caracas) this will be in vol. XVIII.
5. *Obras completas de Andrés Bello*, vol. V (Caracas), pp. 187–8: Critique of Baralt's *Diccionario de galicismos*.
6. ibid., Vol. III, pp. 316–28. In *résumé*, the ideas expressed are: there are two kinds of language, natural and artificial. Natural language (changes of voice, expression and gestures) is formed by association, and must necessarily have preceded artificial language. To explain the formation of

the latter there is no need to imagine some 'formal agreement'; natural language became more and more simplified and evolved into artificial language by means of analogies and similarities giving rise in certain cases to 'a sort of choice, which, made by chance by some individual and adopted by others, constituted a tacit pact whose preliminaries were mediated by nature'. 'A similar process led to writing.' There follows a logical account of the passage from painting to writing and its various phases – enigmatic, tropic, writing on wax, ideographic, phonetic and simplified phonetic. The whole evolution of language, then, resolves itself into 'a series of elementary inventions, each of which cost an almost imperceptible effort of attention and mind, and yet which was the work of centuries. We owe languages not to the meditations nor the genius of exceptional individuals who created them and raised them to their present state, but to the general perfectibility of the human race, to the ability to transmit and accumulate ideas.'

7. ibid., vol. IV, p. 7.
8. ibid., vol. V, p. 6.
9. ibid., vol. IV, p. 9.
10. ibid., vol. III, p. 594. 'Juicio sobre el *Curso de filosofía*, por NOREA'.
11. *Obras completas de Andrés Bello*, vol. VIII (Santiago), p. 314: Bello's speech on his installation as Rector of the University.
12. ibid., p. 423: memorandum to the university, 1854.
13. *Obras completas de Andrés Bello*, Caracas, vol. IX p. 243: Heredia; p. 203: Cienfuegos.
14. ibid., p. 400.
15. ibid., p. 204: 'Juicio sobre Cienfuegos'.
16. ibid., vol. V, p. 193.
17. ibid., vol. VI, p. 5.
18. ibid., vol. VI, p. 333.
19. ibid., p. 127.
20. Amunátegui, op. cit., p. 426.
21. *Obras completas de Andrés Bello*, vol. V (Caracas), p. 102.
22. ibid., p. 83.
23. An idea of the heated discussion raised by the reform of spelling proposed by Bello can be gained from the interesting books of Miguel Luis Amunátegui Reyes, *La reforma ortográfica ante nuestros poderes públicos, ante la Real Academia y ante el buen sentido* (Santiago: 1918), and *Ortografía razonada* (Santiago: 1926).
24. *Obras completas de Andrés Bello*, vol. V (Caracas), p. 93.
25. ibid., p. 121.
26. ibid., pp. cxxxvi–cxxxviii.
27. Bello says in the Prologue to the first edition, 1841: 'I have decided to bring this little work out of the darkness where I had left it buried for over thirty years.' (ibid., p. 7.) So far no one has brought forward sufficient evidence to disprove the scholar's open affirmation.
28. ibid., p. 8.
29. Resolution of the IV Congreso de Academias de la Langua Castellana, Buenos Aires, 1964.

30. *Boletín de la Academia Nacional de la Historia* (Caracas), no. 51 (July–September 1930), p. 295.

31. Menéndez y Pelayo, op. cit., p. cxxvii.

32. *Obras completas de Andrés Bello*, vol. VI (Caracas), p. 368. 'The declinable nouns in Castilian have four cases: the nominative, the accusative complementary, the dative complementary and, finally, a case which never signifies a complement by itself; but which needs an anterior preposition, which by itself means nothing but the end of some complement, and to which can very properly be applied the name of terminal, as the name of complementaries is given to *me*, *les* and *los*.'

33. ibid., vol. V, p. 235.

34. The work was published under the title: *Gramática castellana. Obra inédita, dada a luz con un prólogo y anotaciones, por Miguel Luis Amunátegui* (n.d.).

35. *Obras completas de Andrés Bello*, vol. IV (Caracas), pp. 11–12. Note the golden mean which Bello follows between the ambiguous meanings which he condemns here and the new metaphorical meaning which he praises before.

36. Orrego Vicuña mentions in his work the favourable opinions of Cañete, Menéndez y Pelayo, Marco Fidel Suárez, Rufino José Cuervo, Amunátegui, Barros Arana, Sandalio Letelier, Conde de la Viñaza, Balbín de Unquera and Saavedra, as well as the critical ones of Zorobabel Rodríguez, op. cit., pp. 126ff, 303ff.

37. Quoted by Amunátegui, op. cit., p. 593.

38. Menéndez y Pelayo, op. cit., p. 126.

39. Amunátegui, op. cit., pp. 541–3.

40. *Obras completas de Andrés Bello*, vol. IV (Caracas), pp. ix, lxxxvi.

4 *The Educationist*

Bello's educational work until he went to Chile was incidental. It is true that he taught: in Caracas he was a tutor for a time, and in London his teaching helped to pay for the bitter bread of exile. But until he settled in Chile this activity, the most fruitful of his life, was no more than a means of earning his living or a makeshift occupation. The classes he gave in Caracas when he was a philosophy student, as a way of paying for his studies, did not arouse his enthusiasm, and his lack of economic success turned him against ever teaching again in Venezuela. From this excursion the only thing he gained was the lasting satisfaction of having contributed to the education of his contemporary Bolívar. There are stories of the lessons he gave in London, but nothing leads us to believe that they left any deep trace.

In contrast, in Chile teaching comes to the forefront of his life. Bello's work in his second mother-land has passed into history as a Herculean labour of education. He educated, rather than merely taught. He instilled knowledge into the minds of young Chileans, but he did much more: he trained men by word and by example, and came to be the educator of a whole people through his leadership of its stoutest intellectual vanguard.[1]

Bello was 48 years old when he arrived in the south. His life of arduous and constant study had made him an exceptionally learned man. Convinced that education is the foundation of all progress, and wishing to make the best possible response to the hospitality he received, he at once began teaching as a professor. The Colegio de Santiago, his first foundation in Chile, lasted only a short time; but he continued to teach in his own house, giving classes in natural and international law, Latin, Roman law, grammar and literature, and philosophy. He also taught in the Instituto Nacional, and when the University of Chile was established by a law which he had drafted, he became its Rector until after his death, because no successor was named for some time. The press was for him a living, daily Chair. His *Cosmo-*

graphy, his great speeches at this installation and the anniversaries of the foundation of the university, his *Principios del derecho de gentes*, *Filosofía del entendimiento* and *Gramática castellana*, were all produced as a part of his educational work.

To speak of Bello as an educationalist, in fact, is to summarise all of his many-sided work. Each of his separate activities has a second significance, in education. Therefore, rather than give in this chapter a detailed account of Bello's educational work, I intend to present a synthesis of his general ideas on educational problems.

THE COMPLETE EDUCATION

Balance is the key-note of Bello's educational ideas: intellectual, moral and physical education, all at work on the pupil at the same time, must bring the orderly development of all his faculties.

The complete education which he preached was like the one he himself received – profound, intelligible and laborious. A profound education is the indispensable basis of any intellectual life. The teacher must instil the fundamental principles which rule human knowledge, and teach their application to the various fields of investigation. In this way the pupil will be able, like Bello, to assimilate a multiplicity of facts in such a way that they form a solid construction and not a disordered and incoherent hoard. Education must be intelligible,[2] because 'it is not a good foundation for mental discipline to accustom the mind to be satisfied with words which mean nothing to it';[3] but without taking to harmful extremes the desire to make the child understand what he is being taught. And finally, education must be laborious and prepare the pupil for effort and persistence. 'It is necessary for the child to understand what he is learning; but it may be harmful to him to make the acquisition of his first lessons too easy at every step. He must not be made into a passive receptacle of the ideas of others, to which he need add nothing. He should be accustomed from the start to struggle against difficulties.'[4]

Some have succeeded in banishing from education the wearisomeness which is natural to it, by showing to the children in their lessons objects of pleasure and diversion; but simply by doing this they have succeeded in banishing the love of work, which must be instilled from the very start, and have created frivolous minds, giving them such a superficial training that after a few years it only leaves shameful evidence of the time lost. A boy's first lessons should be too deep to produce at once mature fruit, but they should be very deliberate and well organised so that they are permanent. They should not fill the boy's brains with scraps of many fields of knowledge, the very bulk of which stuns his tender understanding, nor should they force him to attend a series of compulsory classes so long that they keep him in a state of apprenticeship for half his life.[5]

The intellectual education that Bello suggests should develop the spirit of observation, since 'a training which does not try to increase and develop observation and other commendable faculties cannot be complete, nor can it produce the slightest benefit in the future;'[6] and it should be broad, since 'the best education of the mind, that which is of most help in the inquiry after truth in learning and in the business of life, is that which from the start calls into play all the intellectual faculties'.[7]

But this education is not sufficient. Religious and moral education were in the forefront of Bello's mind when he wrote: 'Morality (which I do not separate from religion) is the very life of society';[8] and Bello's life was one long lesson in morality. So it is no surprise to hear him say: 'The principles of our religion cannot but take the first place: without them we should have no standard for our actions, a standard which, reining in the wayward impulses of our hearts, allows us to fulfil our duties to God, to men, and to ourselves.'[9] Or again: 'Above all, the encouragement of the religious and moral education of the people is a duty imposed on every member of the university by the fact of being accepted into its bosom.'[10] Referring to primary and secondary education, Bello asserted: 'Religious instruction is the subject to which the Senate of the university pays the most thorough and constant attention in the reports and statements which it regularly received on primary and secondary education.'[11] And as for the teachers' training college, he complains that religion is not given 'the attention desirable in an institution intended to spread wholesome ideas throughout the territory of the Republic, ideas the lack of which is truly lamentable in almost all districts'.[12] I feel that the quotations need no commentary.

I should, however, like to make it clear that the religious and moral education which Bello desired was not merely some knowledge of religion and ethics. On the contrary, he wanted every child to be taught conviction of his religious and moral duty, and for this to be supported by careful encouragement of his feelings. He hoped to make religion and morality felt by the people, not relegated to the class of forgotten things, and even less to that of superstitious practices. This is why, in an article entitled 'Comercio de libros', he bemoaned the small sale of prayerbooks for a true, spiritual congregation at the rites of the Catholic Church; for, as he says, 'what is bodily presence without the common spiritual presence of thought and emotion, which is the very soul of the established religion?' 'Or do we feel that the intentions of the church are accomplished when the impression which she has attempted to make on our souls has gone no farther than our ears, which perhaps it never reaches?'[13]

The man who, in his youth, 'sometimes alone, sometimes with friends, crossed the valleys, rested on the banks of the rivers, climbed the mountains', and went on various expeditions with Humboldt;[14] the man who 'was endowed with a physique which, although not apparently athletic, was strong and perfectly normal'; this man did not ever neglect physical education.[15] Indeed, Bello recognised the importance of physical education 'which inspired souls with noble and generous feelings', as one of the causes of 'the flourishing Greek civilisation'.[16]

In Bello's educational design welfare and happiness are united. 'Our aim in training men's minds and hearts is to seek benefits and avoid unhappiness for each one; and therefore we may consider education as the use of those faculties of man which are most appropriate for the advance of human well-being.'[17]

ALL BRANCHES OF EDUCATION

Certain other observations of the Venezuelan scholar should be pondered by those who wish to work in the educational field.

For example, the following statement concerning secondary education is not inapplicable today:

I shall never cease to repeat a general observation which has been made before about secondary education, and whose importance is such that it must be rubbed in. Generally the subjects of this level of education are thought of as being merely preparations for professional careers; that is, they are considered simply as a means and not as an end important in itself. From this general point of view spring serious disadvantages for the spread of intellectual civilisation. Those who do not aim at a learned profession do not appreciate the true value of the possession of this knowledge, which is everywhere a mark of cultivation in men; and it must be confessed that this lack is often noted in that class which is most favoured by fortune, among whom should most notably be found that grace and elegance which stem from a cultivated intelligence and are typical of a society in progress. And so these preparatory studies are carried out without real diligence or liking, as indispensable conditions which open the door to knowledge not more advanced but more lucrative; as intellectual acquisitions which for those who have attained them are not worth keeping up, and of which few traces are seen in the course of life. Another consequence of this feeling is that few young people attend the secondary schools in the provinces, which are mainly intended to spread that light which no man of normal education should lack and which prepare him not only for social intercourse but to fulfil reasonably those functions which are obligatory to all citizens in our political organisation.[18]

Bello also defended the teaching of Latin: 'The teaching of the native language and of Latin', he wrote, 'is the foundation stone of all learning.' 'The continual occupation in comparing two different instruments with which the same thought is expressed accustoms the young man from early days to meditation, which is so essential to lead him on to higher and more profound ideas.'[19]

To encourage the study of Latin, Bello published a corrected and finished edition of the *Gramática latina* by his son Francisco, who died when he was just beginning to become productive. Such is the character of Bello's work in this that the *Gramática latina*, based on the second and later editions, is incorporated in the *Obras completas de Andrés Bello*, after serious consideration by the Editorial Commission.[20]

ANDRÉS BELLO AND PRIMARY EDUCATION

It is scarcely worth saying that Andrés Bello was in favour of primary education. 'But', he adds, 'for that very reason I believe that it is very necessary to encourage literary and scientific education.' Primary education flourishes only 'where the arts and sciences are already in a flourishing state'. He does not say that primary education is the consequence of higher education, but that it needs this higher stage in order to develop: 'Good schoolmasters, good books, good direction of studies are necessarily the fruit of a very advanced intellectual culture.'[21]

As the most appropriate means of the encouragement of primary education, he enthusiastically promoted the teachers' training college (escuela normal). As he said: 'Without this college, all the measures which might be taken to spread primary education would be, at the least, inefficient, because the first element would always be lacking, and without any doubt that is the supply of good and upright masters.'[22] The education which these institutions should provide ought to have as its object the training of good school-teachers; and of course it should aim to make them adequate not merely for intellectual teaching, but also for the moral and religious training of their pupils.[23]

It is completely unjust to say that Bello, in his zeal for higher education, would place primary education on a lower plane. In his annual memoranda to the university he always reported on the progress of primary education, which was under his care. He thought of 'general education, the education of the people, as one of the most important and exceptional objectives to which the Government could give its attention; as a prime and urgent need, being the basis of all sound progress; as the indispensable foundation of our republican institutions'. Simply to mention Bello's interest in the training of future schoolmasters through the teachers' training college should suffice to designate him as one of the most upright and concerned promoters of education for the people. Without teachers there is no education of the people. And, as Orrego Vicuña has said, he was 'the first in Chile, and possibly in Spanish America, to favour the establishment of teachers' training colleges'.[24] However, there remains a most vivid memory of Bello's view that the university must retain the oversight of all levels of education and of the emphasis he placed on the need to develop a sound training as the basis for the spread of education. Lastarria, like Sarmiento, urged priority for education of the people, believing that a flourishing university culture was the consequence of the spread of education. The educational battlefields of Spanish America re-echo the cries of both sides.[25] Nevertheless, both sides are agreed on the need for urgent attention and unselfish encouragement in education. If we could complement this with Bello's manifest interest in secondary education, we should see his concept of the total education of man shine once again, despite the clouds of speech-making.[26]

The truth is that Bello practised, and also embraced, the educationalist's noble ideal of the complete education, from primary school to university. Also, it is true, he regarded the university as the originator and director of all preparatory studies. Bello was Rector of the University of Chile, but as such he was also chairman of a university Senate which had the duty of supervising preliminary instruction throughout the country. He sought to unite, as he did in other aspects of his life, the theoretical principles with the effects in practice. But this swift review of Bello's ideas on education must not turn us away from a consideration of Bello as the teacher in the harsh field of life. If it is true that he conceived a system of complete education, he nevertheless had the uncommon merit of giving himself, day after day, to the task of training men to study for the good of all, of awakening and directing inquiring thoughts. Bello's life, especially after his arrival in Chile, was given over to continual, persevering educational work. Education is not just one aspect of Bello's work: it is his whole life. Amunátegui has written the shortest and most complete summary of Bello's life, almost an epitaph: 'We can say, without a lie, that Bello spent his life teaching.'[27]

CHAPTER 4: NOTES AND REFERENCES

1. 'Among all the tasks which Bello carried out in his long and fruitful life, on behalf of the culture of Chile and of Spanish America, none was so important or of such great and continuing effect, as the foundation of the University of Chile.' (Orrego Vicuña, *Don Andrés Bello*, p. 193.)

2. For this reason he wrote in the Foreword to his *Gramática para uso de las escuelas*: 'In the definitions we have not attempted rigorous exactness. Rather we have tried to point out objects, as with the finger, than to explain them in precise formulas, which are rarely understood by the intelligence of children.' *Obras completas de Andrés Bello*, vol. V (Caracas), p. 235.

3. *Obras completas de Andrés Bello*, vol. VIII (Santiago), p. 377. Speech on the anniversary of the foundation of the university.

4. *Obras completas de Andrés Bello*, vol. III (Caracas), p. 530.

5. *Obras completas de Andrés Bello*, vol. VIII (Santiago), p. 191: 'Observaciones sobre el plan de estudios que ha formado la Comisión nombrada por el Supremo Gobierno en 1832.'

6. Letter to Irisarri, London, 11 September 1820. In Guillermo Feliú Cruz, 'Bello, Irisarri y Egaña en Londres', reproduced in *Boletín de la Academia Nacional de la Historia* (Caracas), no. 40 (October–December 1927), pp. 324ff. This study was included in Feliú's book *Andrés Bello y la redacción de los documentos oficiales administrativos, internacionales, ye legislativos de Chile* (Caracas: 1957). This letter is on p. 25.

7. *Obras completas de Andrés Bello*, vol. III (Caracas), p. 529.

8. *Obras completas de Andrés Bello*, vol. VIII (Santiago), p. 304.

9. ibid., p. 218: 'Educación'.

10. ibid., p. 310: speech on his installation as Rector of the University. See also p. 311 and p. 367: 'Speech on the anniversary of the university', 1848; and p. 413: memorandum presented to the university, 1854.

11. ibid., p. 367: speech on the anniversary of the university, 1848.

12. ibid., p. 406: memorandum to the university, 1854.

13. ibid., vol. XIII, p. 330. The Bible which Bello used in London, with his personal notes, is in the Seminary of Santiago, where his son Juan Bello Dunn deposited it.

14. Amunátegui, op. cit., p. 21.

15. *Obras completas de Andrés Bello*, vol. IV (Santiago), p. xxxi: speech of the Dean of the faculty of humanities of the University of Chile, Francisco de Vargas Fontecilla, on the first centenary of Bello's birth.

16. *Obras completas de Andrés Bello*, vol. IX (Caracas), p. 37: *Historia de la literatura.*

17. *Obras completas de Andrés Bello*, vol. VIII (Santiago), p. 213: 'Educación).

18. ibid., p. 142: memorandum to the Senate of the university, 11 March 1854.

19. ibid., pp. 192–3. He also brought forward other arguments: 1. 'It is difficult to speak Castilian correctly if one does not know its mother-language.' 2. 'Nor is there anything which makes the acquisiton of foreign languages more easy than a previous knowledge of Latin.' 3. 'For the cultivation of letters nothing is more important than Latin.' 4. 'Latin is the language of the religion we profess.' 5. 'There is almost no subject of science which does not benefit from the knowledge of the Classical languages, since their nomenclature is almost all Latin or Greek.' (*Obras completas de Andrés Bello*, vol. VIII (Caracas), pp. 489–91: 'Latin y derecho romano'.)

20. ibid. See explanation of this editorial decision, in the Introduction by Father Aurelio Espinosa Pólit, pp. xiff.

21. *Obras completas de Andrés Bello*, vol. VIII (Santiago), p. 309–10: speech on his installation as Rector of the University.

22. ibid., p. 262: 'Escuela Normal'.

23. ibid., p. 407.

24. *Don Andrés Bello*, p. 120.
25. For example see the repercussion of the debate between Bello and Lastarria in the book of the Chilean Dean Galdames, *La universidad autónoma* (San José, Costa Rica: 1935), pp. 12ff.
26. Note here that, complementary to Bello's interest in primary education, he encouraged the establishment of Sunday schools for labourers.
27. Amunátegui, op. cit., p. 351.

5 *The Jurist*

Driven by family tradition and by his own inclination, Bello studied law in Caracas.[1] But Amunátegui says: 'His father, although a good lawyer, seems for some reason which I do not know, to have found the profession distasteful,' and 'Don Andrés, on his part, had inherited from his father an aversion to the somewhat unattractive contests of the litigants, and so he felt he had no vocation to spend his life becoming involved with them'.[2] Bello's distaste for the exercise of the profession of law is explained by his character, which allowed him no enjoyment of controversies outside the field of learning, and which also kept him apart from these professional disputes, as well as, almost entirely, from political involvement. So he felt dislike for the courts, but keen interest for the study of jurisprudence. And this interest, based on his sound training in Caracas, led to his acquisition of exceptional knowledge of the law, which in turn enabled him to offer solutions in all branches of the field. Amunátegui says that in Chile, Bello, for economic reasons, decided to 'obtain the legal title to defend cases', and that as a first step he graduated on the 17 September 1836 as Bachelor of Canon and Civil Law. But then he decided not to become fully qualified 'though this would have given him no trouble at all; nor to practise the profession, which would have ensured him a lucrative income. But, if he had no vocation to be a lawyer, he certainly had one to become a jurist.'[3] This fortunate phrase of Bello's biographer and pupil exactly defines Bello the jurist.

Bello taught various legal subjects, and he also took a leading part in the extensive work of legislation which was accomplished in Chile during the years he lived there. He was prompt in the defence of the rights of the Chilean State in the international disputes which were referred to him, and was the inspiration of the Chilean Government's actions from his post of Principal Officer in the Ministry of Foreign Relations. He also wrote various legal textbooks and gave opinions on many legal inquiries made by private citizens.

In this chapter I shall try to summarise Bello's writings and main ideas on law.

A PHILOSOPHICAL CONCEPT OF LAW

I must begin by saying that Bello condemns the mechanical study of law as the mere art of applying and interpreting positive statutes: his whole life was one long protest against this kind of juridical pragmatism. He wrote:

We should like to see the study of jurisprudence itself broadened and dignified; to see the young lawyer extending his scope beyond the limited and uncertain field of Court practice, deepening the philosophical principles of this noble science, and studying it in its relationship with the eternal bases of justice and the common good. But he should not forget to temper his severity, making it more agreeable by diligent cultivation of philosophy and the humanities, without which there has never been an eminent jurist.[4]

He supported, then, the study of the philosophy of law, on which he gave classes under the heading of natural law,[5] and prepared a textbook on the subject, of which the Prologue to Volume IX of his *Obras* (Santiago edition) contains two pages in Bello's own hand, given by his pupil Manuel Antonio Tocornal to Amunátegui. These pages are reproduced as an appendix to Volume XIV of the Caracas edition of the *Obras completas*, which is concerned with Roman law.[6]

Bello's treatise on international law gave him the opportunity to study various points of juridical philosophy: the division of law into subjective and objective and the subdivisions,[7] the sanction, including moral and religious sanctions,[8] and especially the existence of rational natural law, immutable, eternal, primary with respect to positive law, and which he defends against 'various authors, who deny absolutely the existence of a true law, obligatory of itself and independent of the human will; for according to them there are no laws save those promulgated by the material power of the rulers as being vested with a divine mission of domination'.[9]

The following statement concerning the existence of natural law deserves to be read:

All law supposes an authority from which it flows. Since nations do not depend upon each other, the laws or rules which regulate their conduct towards each other can only be laid down by reason, which, in the light of experience, and consulting the common good, deduces them from the linking of causes and effects which we perceive in the physical and moral order of the universe. The Supreme Being, who has established these causes and effects, who has placed in man an irresistible desire for good or happiness and does not allow us to sacrifice the happiness of others to our own, is therefore the true author of these laws, and reason does nothing more than interpret them.[10]

From the columns of *El araucano*, Bello also defended natural law as the basis of international law, against an article which denied 'that there are rules of international law which, without the previous consent of nations, nevertheless compel them'.

Here we see that perfect international law does not exist, and that the pretended human code which rules all societies is the vaguest, most indefinite and most imperfect thing. But the fact that the international code dictated only by nature is imperfect, does it indeed prove that, speaking absolutely, there is no such code? It is true that many of the rules of international morality are vague and indefinite; but not all of them are, nor does the fact that a rule is indefinite or vague, that it is too general or abstract, suppose that it cannot be applied clearly and evidently to very many cases. It is true that often these rules are applied wrongly, but this is an argument against the application, not against the rules. . . . The abuse of international law, based on the nature of man and his societies, is a proof of its existence. The very men who twist it recognise it.[11]

Also, in another piece written about this same polemic there appears this paragraph, which completes the definition of Bello's views on international law: 'But that law laid down by good sense, immutable, eternal, whom does it compel? Without any doubt it compels men; and not only men considered as individuals, but groups of men, towns and States, in their reciprocal relations.'[12] With respect to the problem of codification, Bello was a convinced supporter and practiser of it, but he avoided the extremism, which was still very much the fashion, of making laws on a purely rational basis, without taking notice of the social reality. Bello, on the contrary, always took great care to consult custom in his legislative work, and never thought of codes as being immutable and eternal. The influence of English examples and his reading of Savigny cured him of all wishful thinking. Categorical, indeed, is the statement in the message with which the President of the Republic and the Minister of Justice forwarded to the Chilean Congress the draft of the Civil Code which Bello had prepared – a message which, rightfully, is included in Bello's *Obras*:

Many of the most civilised modern nations have felt the need to codify their laws. It can be said that this is a periodic need of societies. However complete and perfect a body of laws may appear to be, the changes in customs, the very progress of civilisation, political vicissitudes, the entry of new ideas, leading to new institutions, scientific discoveries and their applications to the arts and practical life, the abuses introduced by bad faith, always inventive of means of evading legal precautions, all these things ceaselessly stimulate new measures which are added to the former ones, interpreting, modifying and repealing them, until at length it becomes necessary to revise this confused mass of diverse, incoherent and contradictory elements, giving them consistency and order and bringing them into step with the living forms of the social order.[13]

These 'living forms of the social order' get him round his concept of law, the rationalist view of natural law, for which reason had to be the sole and decisive source of law. On the contrary, Bello, by recognising that law lives, and changes as social life changes, was able to reconcile the idea of a rigid natural law with the idea of contingency and changeability which a historical viewpoint has always recognised in juridical life.

Don Andrés Bello's philosophical knowledge of law was manifest in his solution of many juridical problems.[14] In him, as in Savigny, the great model of his century, philosophy presided over the work of the jurist and of the legislator.

ROMAN LAW, THE JURIST'S TRAINING GROUND

Knowing Bello's leaning towards the deep study of the whole vast legal field, his interest in Roman law is scarcely surprising; and if, from the press, he defended the study of Roman law for its formative nature as well as for its practical utility – as the source and also as a model which explained and supplemented

Spanish law, still at that time in force in Chile[15] – his work for this subject was of greater importance in the university. 'The university, I make so bold as to say,' ran his speech at his installation there, 'will not welcome that preconception which condemns the study of Roman law as useless or pernicious; I believe that, on the contrary, it will give the subject fresh encouragement or will set it on a broader base.'[16]

In his speech on the anniversary of the university in 1848 he made some interesting statements emphasising his point of view.

I should wish, Gentlemen, the study of Roman jurisprudence to be more extensive and deep. For me this is fundamental. . . . Our object is the training of the scholarly jurist; his apprenticeship in that special logic so necessary for the interpretation and application of the laws, and which forms the character which distinguishes so especially the jurisprudence of the Romans. . . . Nor do I think there is any need to refute the prejudice of those who ignore the practical usefulness of Roman law, particularly in countries whose civil law is derived from Roman law, and is almost a copy of it. It is enough to say that never has it been more highly regarded, nor has its study been more generally recommended, even from the point of view of judicial and court practice. I shall quote, from Savigny, the example of the French jurists who, he says, use Roman law with great skill to illustrate and complete their civil code, so acting according to the spirit of that same code.[17]

Here once again the aims of the educationalist lead him to the production of a book. He remarks the need of 'a more comprehensive and substantial textbook', and settles to the task of providing one. Amunátegui says:

With this purpose in mind, Don Andrés Bello enriched Heineccius's text with important corrections, numerous additions and explanatory notes, the material for which he drew from civil law and its most famous commentators. The little compendium grew in this way into a great work, which I have seen partly in manuscript and part printed by the printing works managed by Bello's son Don Andrés Ricardo Bello and Don Felipe Santiago Matta.[18]

The Amunáteguis did not include Bello's writings on Roman law in the first edition of his *Obras*: they simply printed the Foreword in the Introduction to the *Opúsculos jurídicos*. The various works which Bello prepared for the use of his students of Roman law constitute Volume XIV of the Caracas edition of the *Obras completas*, with a solid Prologue by Hessel E. Yntema, Professor of Comparative Law in the University of Michigan.

In his memorandum to the university of 1859 Bello returned to the theme of the need to broaden the study of Roman law. The fact is worth noting, since already by that date the Civil Code which he had written for Chile had been promulgated. It was not, therefore, the lack of a civil code which had caused him to deepen and extend the study of Roman law. And here he repeated, amongst his main arguments, that of the usefulness in the lawyer's training of Roman logic, 'so strict in its deductions that the great Leibnitz did not hesitate to compare it with the process of mathematical reasoning'.[19]

WRITING ON ALL BRANCHES OF LAW

Bello's legal productivity will fill seven volumes of the Caracas *Obras completas*, without including his work in the Chilean Senate[20] and the messages and government papers,[21] which in a way might be considered as Bello's activities in connection with the organisation of the Chilean civil service. Two volumes are allotted to the draft Civil Code,[22] and three to international law;[23] but other volumes are splendidly invaded by all the branches of law.

Bello dealt with political law when, in his *Principios de derecho de gentes*, he expounded the basic questions of sovereignty, its forms and most important consequences (among them territory, authority and citizenship), and when, putting a beneficial stop to the excesses of the theory of the separation of powers, he nevertheless praised the independence of the judicial power, although clarifying its unavoidable relations with the other powers:

But since in these functions the judge does nothing more than prepare for the execution of the laws, the person who is in charge of this branch of the constitutional powers should examine carefully the ways those functionaries who apply the laws carry out their task, not to destroy the independence of judges by correcting the abuses which may have been committed in each particular case, but to guard against abuses which might be committed in future, to make whoever should commit them responsible, to watch beneficially over the inviolability of the laws, whose observance is entrusted to their care. . . . If the executive attempts, we will not say to dictate a judicial decision, but even to incline to one side or the other the opinions of the judges in a case, the executive will commit a culpable usurpation of authority, violating the independence of the courts; but if the executive follows the proceedings in this or that contentious case or in all of them at once, if it tries to investigate the state in which they are in order to know whether the judicial duties are being scrupulously carried out, if it examines the conduct of the officers who have in their charge the branch of the state which is the most vital for the preservation and order of society, then the executive, far from committing an abuse, will have fulfilled one of the most sacred obligations imposed on it by the constitution, the justice and the interests of the Republic.[24]

Bello gave opinions on many questions of administrative law: he showed the need for Chile to empower as many ports and harbours as possible to take part in coastal trade, and in general to bring the greatest development to administrative law concerning sea-borne traffic; he defended the agreement for the construction of the railway between Santiago and Valparaíso; he advocated the adoption of the metric system; he succeeded in having abolished as useless the parliamentary custom of replying to the opening speech of the President of the Republic; he supported the Bill to establish the national General Archive; he proposed to reform the law concerning authors' copyrights, and for this purpose he made a study of similar laws in the principal countries. I believe that this brief exposition will be enough to give an idea of the breadth of his work in this respect.

We also find Bello grappling with varied problems of penal law in his legal work. The influence of Jeremy Bentham is clear. Bello defends the social usefulness of penalties;[25] but in Bello's eclectic views and his classical philosophy shone the superior notion of the righting of the wrong done.

With regard to the prison system, which should be guided by the double aim of the penalty's usefulness – reform of the criminal and giving an example to society – Bello criticised the system in use in Chile and proposed reforms based on experiments carried out in the United States.

He criticised severely the abuse of the law of reprieve, since he thought that 'anything which diminishes the certainty of the penalty, diminishes its efficacy as a guard against crime. To allow those who are tempted to commit a crime to have in their minds the probability of a reprieve is truly to induce them to commit it; and this is the tendency of arbitrary reprieves. . . .'[26] 'Let it not be thought', he says, 'that we wish to take away from the supreme magistrate of the Republic sentiments of compassion nor generous acts of clemency, and there is no citizen in whom these should shine more brightly. We only wish that such acts should go hand in hand with justice, for without this virtue all the others are merely fanciful; and badly understood clemency is in fact cruelty, all the more harmful the more it is covered up.[27]

Bello considered that the publication of verdicts of guilty or not guilty was a great social influence, serving as an example in the case of guilty, and in the case of not guilty serving to clear the reputations of accused who are found innocent. He published with warm approval the provisions of the Penal Code of Louisiana concerning 'offenses which affect the reputation';[28] in his draft Civil Code he defended the existence of extenuating circumstances with respect to the consequences of divorce (*quoad thorum*) where the guilt of the condemned spouse was extenuated by serious circumstances in the conduct of the spouse granted the divorce; and with regard to adultery, he advocated the punishment only of incest and similar crimes, because of the advisability of 'erasing absolutely this class of crimes from the list of those which should be subject to human justice', claiming that 'there are social ills whose cure is a matter for religion and morality alone'.[29]

Bello did not neglect commercial law. In 1835 he was nominated, together with four other persons, to constitute the Commission set up to study the Spanish Commercial Code and report to the Government 'on the changes which it believes should be made in it, with the object of submitting it for the approval of the legislature'. Bello himself had proposed this in an article in *El araucano*, but he was unable to take charge of the writing and could only offer to co-operate in the work, and the Commission did not meet again.[30] Bello wrote about commercial law in many articles, and in his *Principios de derecho internacional*,

while studying mercantile traffic between nations, he made a
concise summary of the history of commercial law.

One of Bello's greatest concerns was procedural law, for he
regarded the administration of justice as the foundation stone
of the social order.

Security, property, honour, indeed everything that man seeks and
finds in society is based precisely on the honest administration of
justice. Without this the laws are a vain pretence, for it does not
matter that they exist and are the best if bad application or lack of
observance nullifies them, or if, in order to gain their effect, a man
has to suffer greater evils than those which obliged him to ask for
their fulfilment.[31]

Bello carried on an intensive campaign to have every sentence
given out together with the reasons for the judge's decision; he
strove to have verdicts published (except those relating to sexual
honour), which would bring as consequences greater truthful-
ness and honesty in witnesses, greater spread of knowledge of the
law, an effective moral sanction which would prompt and curb
the judges; he proposed that in courts with panels of judges
each question should be voted on separately and a distinction
should be made between fact and law; he supported (a reflection
of an age which preferred certainty to speed) the need for a third
appeal in the case of two contradictory decisions. Bello also
suggested the abolition of the swearing in of witnesses, since 'with
religious and moral witnesses there is no risk of suppressing the
oath; with irreligious witnesses there is a real advantage in its
suppression';[32] he introduced in matters of proof the need for
written documents in all contracts of more than a certain sum;
and he emphasised the importance of presumption or con-
jecture in legal proof.

Bello's articles on notaries were vivid and very real criticisms
of the carelessness, faults and negligence in the mechanical part
of the administration of justice. Also the theme of obedience to
the law gave him the opportunity to point out abuses in the
judicial system, such as intercession with the judge outside
court proceedings, and visits of the parties to the judge, and he
advised: 'Let the judge hear the case in the public place designated for the trial; this is his duty; but outside it, let him hear

nothing, for his mind will be open to surprise, and because it is essential that those who seek justice should realise that they will not obtain it by fulfilling many formalities but by proceeding in all things wihout leaving the road which the law had laid down.'[33] In the question of whether to have one or several judges, Bello sided with Bentham:

One alone is preferable to several [because] as Bentham says, singleness of judicature is favourable to all the circumstances which should be demanded in a judge, whereas plurality diminishes and weakens them. The integrity of a judge depends greatly on his responsibility; and his responsibility is much greater whether before the law or with respect to public opinion (which is after all the sole court which can exercise effective supervision over a judge, when he is provided with the means to investigate and to pronounce his judgements), if it weighs on one man alone, and if that man has no other support before the public than the rectitude of his decisions, nor any other shield than the esteem of his fellow citizens and if, were he to commit an injustice, the whole discredit would fall on him, and he would be alone against the universal indignation. Few men sacrifice themselves for virtue, none for infamy. Even if a judge were not upright by inclination, he would have to be, despite himself, in a situation in which his interest is evidently inseparable from his duty.[34]

Finally, Bello advocated the codification of the laws of court procedure. In the memorandum which he presented to the Congress of 1855, the Minister of Justice expressed the hope that 'the industrious jurist to whom we owe the Civil Code would undertake the Procedural Code'; but Bello, now an old man, was not able to fulfil the task.[35]

All the ideas which I have tried to systematise above are spread throughout Bello's work:[36] the only juridical books of his which remain, and which therefore demand somewhat more careful attention, are the *Principios de derecho internacional* and the *Código Civil.*

FOUNDER OF LATIN AMERICAN INTERNATIONAL LAW

The birth of the Spanish American nations to independent life brought the need for their jurists to deepen their study of international law. The New States, little developed in themselves and exhausted by the wars of emancipation, needed to possess a clear idea of their rights and their defensive arguments in order to make their legal situation prevail in conflicts with powers provided with incomparably superior means, when they could not satisfactorily guarantee victory by force.

Bello, who must already have possessed the first notions of international law when he left Venezuela, broadened his knowledge considerably during his diplomatic career. Faced with obvious problems, he studied the opinions of the best authorities of the day on international law and the practical applications which international legal standards had had in the lives of the nations. Once he was in Chile, he entered the service of the Ministry of Foreign Relations and gave private classes in international law. This teaching was the immediate cause of the publication of his *Principios de derecho de gentes*, whose first edition came out in 1832. The *Principios de derecho de gentes* has received much high praise from authoritative writers; but in order to gain some idea of its importance it will suffice to recall how many editions it has gone through. In Chile, in Don Andrés's lifetime, a second impression was made in 1844 and a third in 1864, both improved: in the second appeared the author's name, which before had been modestly represented by the initials A.B., and the title was changed to *Principios de derecho internacional*, 'a name which, he thought, tended now to be more used in the language than *Derecho de gentes*'.[37] Since then it has been printed repeatedly: in Lima, Sucre (Bolivia), Bogotá, Paris, Madrid, as well as having suffered highly incorrect, although picturesque, plagiarism.

The Caracas editions of Bello's book on international law deserve particular attention from Venezuelans, since they testify to the high esteem in which their famous fellow-citizen was held in Caracas. The first Caracas edition of the *Principios de derecho de gentes* was made by Don Valentín Espinal in 1837, only five years after the publication of the first edition in Santiago. In the editorial Foreword the interest of that edition was emphasised:

... not only because of the outstanding merit of the work, but also on account of the circumstance that it has been written by a fellow countryman of ours, to whom, in testimony of the special and distinguished regard we have for his learning and talents, we offer this small but sincere tribute, which redounds to the glory of our country.

Let us hope that, in fulfilment of the wishes of the author and of ourselves, these precious principles may be adopted by all the universities of the new American States, and through them our young men may study a subject which is now urgent because of its usefulness and importance.

In 1847, three years after the second Chilean edition, appeared a second Caracas edition, now with the title *Principios de derecho internacional* and with the name of Andrés Bello on the title page. As Prologue, or Foreword, it has a letter from Irisarri, which gives valuable testimony of the thought Bello had put into the work and the Spanish American concern which inspired him:

Certainly Sr Bello has not composed his book in a short time. I know that thirty years ago he was studying the principles of international law, and he was the first to give me proof of the deficiencies of Vattel's work on international law in all matters which concerned the cause of the emancipation of Spanish America, and it was he who taught me the necessity of studying the modern authors. Since then this learned and patriotic Spanish American has occupied himself in this field of study, and we have the fruits before our eyes; and from that time he had the intention of giving us these *Principios de derecho internacional* so that they might become widespread in these Republics and should be of service in the discussion of our affairs with other nations.[38]

The book is an exposition of the basic principles of international law, arising either from natural law, recognised by human reason, or from positive law, as shown in treaties and international customs. It contains public international law and private international law, and includes a manual of diplomacy and a chapter on the consular service. The most authoritative writers of the time were his guide, together with 'long lists of judicial cases collected in Europe and the United States of America, from which, with accuracy and method, he succeeded in extracting the doctrine'.[39]

Considered as a brilliant synthesis of international principles, Bello's work is of immense value and can still be of real use for students of that branch of law. But without any doubt, its most important aspect is that it studies the vital problems of the international situation of Spanish America. The day when we can consider that an Ibero-American school of international law has been established (a school which would doubtless comprise notable specialists who are our contemporaries), an Ibero-American school which is distinguished by its preference for the study of certain problems which interest us most particularly, and for the vigorous defence of certain principles which have a special importance for us because they protect our most essential rights; that day, the best minds of the South American Continent will have to turn their eyes to Andrés Bello, to recognise him as the founder of that school, as the father of the international law common to our native lands.

With regard to general international law, certain points dealt with by Bello deserve mention because of the importance of their content and the excellence and clarity of the form in which they are expounded. These include his firm belief in a natural law as the indisputable basis of international law; his analysis of the problem of just war; and his recognition of Francisco Suárez as 'the first writer of modern times who succeeded in enunciating pure and sound ideas of natural and international law in his treatise *De legibus ac Deo legislatore*, a rectification of history in which he anticipates the modern international lawyers against the dogmatic belief in Grotius as the original father of international law'.[40]

But I repeat, what is of the most interest in the book is the part dealing with the problems which touch us most closely; because, as Bello himself said in 1840 in the pages of *El araucano*, the principles of international law 'have a double importance in Spanish America, where it is necessary to regard them with particular and (if this were possible) superstitious respect, since without them the disturbances which ruin the new Republics would give frequent and plausible pretexts to ambition for intervention and encroachment'.[41] Bello does in fact study the right of a State to be recognised by the others, a necessity which in his time was essential in Spanish America. He emphasises the very limited nature of the reasons justifying the right of intervention, a problem which he also dealt with in the press: 'The interference of one government in the internal affairs of another or others is not a rule but an exception; generally speaking it is illegitimate, it attacks the independence of States. Only particular circumstances of a grave nature, causing imminent and manifest danger, can justify it.'[42] Bello does not deny that the

Spanish American War of Independence was a civil war, indeed he quotes the categorical declaration of Judge Story that 'the United States Government has recognised the existence of a state of war between Spain and her colonies', but he adds: 'From the time that a new State which is formed by a civil war or any other means performs acts of sovereignty, it has a perfect right that nations with which it is not at war should not hinder in any way the exercise of its independence.'[43] Finally, when studying piracy, he expresses himself very strongly against filibusters:

But it must be recognised that filibustering is not included in the definition of piracy according to international law. It is true that it lacks the open authorisation of an established government; although it is notorious that in the cases to which we have alluded these expeditions counted with the physical and moral support of certain peoples; peoples (*proh nefas!*) both civilised and Christian, ready to help and protect them and intercede for them in misfortune.[44]

Bello was in two minds about the meeting of an American Congress. To begin with, he said, 'we looked upon this idea as a beautiful Utopia sterile of practical consequences for Spanish America,' but later the project began to attract him, in the belief that rapprochement itself would be a positive result.

The various sections of Spanish America have until now been too much separated from each other; their common interests urge them to join together; and nothing which might contribute to this great aim is unworthy of the consideration of governments, statesmen and friends of humanity. For us, even a common language is a precious heritage which we must not dissipate. If we were to add to this link that of analogous institutions, that of legislation which recognised substantially the same principles, that of a uniform international law, that of the co-operation of all the States in the conservation of peace and the administration of justice in each (naturally with the recognised and essential restrictions necessary for individual security), would this not be a worthwhile state of things in all respects, to bring about which we should try means much more difficult and expensive than those needed for a meeting of plenipotentiaries?[45]

Bello's judgement wavered then, between the ideal, more or less realisable, on the one hand, and the difficulty of the undertaking on the other; but he decided that at least there should be an attempt to encourage closer relations between the countries.

In a letter to Antonio Leocadio Guzmán, the Venezuelan delegate to the Congress of Lima, he expressed himself later in the same sense, although he was still unconvinced of success.

In Bello's practical work with respect to international juridical order, his inclination to make treaties which were not onerous stood out; and in his newspaper articles he took great care to make it clear that Chile, in the conflict with Peru and Bolivia, had respected the rules of war.

The high esteem with which Bello's approach to international problems was regarded is testified to by his appointment as an arbitrator in the disputes between the United States and Ecuador in 1864 and between Colombia and Peru in 1865, which he was unable to accept because of his age and bad health, which were already taking him towards the grave.

THE CIVIL CODE OF LATIN AMERICA

According to the President of the Chilean Senate, by 1833 or 1834 Bello had already settled to the task of drawing up a draft Civil Code. On the 14 December 1855 this Bill, after a process of preparation which had gone on for more than twenty years, was promulgated by the Chilean Congress as a national law. If we consider what twenty years of constant work means, carried out with the knowledge and character of such a man, it will seem most natural that this legal corpus was recognised as excellent.

During that long period there were many pitfalls and vicissitudes and much discouragement; but Bello had the moral strength to remain unshaken, adopting everything that could help to improve his work without caring from whom it came, and energetically rejecting all suggestions that his undertaking might fail. In the first edition of his *Obras* four drafts were included, marking different stages, and there was also another one which was not printed, and which represents a phase between the third and fourth drafts, since the third draft (1853) was revised twice.[46] In the Caracas edition of the *Obras completas*, with tremendous pains, the definitive version has been annotated with all the variants of all the drafts and even with the notes which Bello himself added to his own printed copy up to the time of his death.[47] This long work could not have been successfully completed if the author had not possessed sufficient breadth of mind to accept any proper observation without clinging to his first ideas, and if he had not worked ceaselessly to improve it, as he did to the extreme that at his death, his copy of the Code was found marked with manuscript observations and emendations which would certainly have provided the material for future revisions.

The representatives of Chilean sovereignty showed their gratitude for the fine present which the scholar gave to their country. Following the President's initiative, the Congress gave Bello a special vote of thanks, the sum of 20,000 pesos and an increment in his years of service to enable him to retire from the staff of the Ministry of Foreign Relations at full salary. And even then, the authorities had the honesty to recognise the insufficiency of this reward. 'For my part', said the President of the Senate, 'I believe that the sum with which we have tried to recompense his work is very small. Sr Bello has not even enjoyed the stipend of 4,000 pesos a year which the executive allotted to the drafters of the legal codes. But, since we have not the power to increase it, it is right that we, on our part, should agree to this scant token of our gratitude.'[48]

The best explanatory synthesis of the general character of the provisions of the Code is the message with which the President of the Chilean Republic and the Minister of Justice forwarded to the Congress the definitive draft in 1855, which is included in Bello's *Obras* because there is no doubt that it was written by the author of the draft himself, judging by its style.[49]

I do not think I need to refute the opinion which it seems was formed at first sight by some, that the Chilean Code is nothing but an adaptation of the best which had been drawn up until then. Today no one denies the originality of Bello's work. Frequently he adopted, but according to a preconceived plan, the things which seemed to him most rational or most fitted to local customs in the other codes. The message quoted takes pains to forestall this criticism: 'Of course you will understand that we did not try to copy word for word any of the modern codes. It was necessary to use them without losing sight of the special circumstances of our country. But where these did not present real obstacles we have not hesitated to introduce beneficial innovations.'[50] The message also foresaw criticism of the large

number of definitions and examples it contains, and explained
the considerations which brought about this apparent excess:

With respect to the method and plan which have been followed in
this Code, I shall remark that the Code could have been made less
voluminous by the omission perhaps of the examples which accompany the abstract rules, or perhaps of the corollaries derived from
these rules, and which were certainly unnecessary for the trained
minds of magistrates and lawyers. But in my opinion we have rightly
followed the opposite practice, in imitation of the wise legislator of
the old *Siete Partidas* [Alfonso X]. The examples bring out the true
meaning and spirit of a law in its applications; and the corollaries
demonstrate what is involved in it, which might escape the less
shrewd eye. In this question brevity seemed to be a secondary
consideration.[51]

Bello's numerous smaller writings on civil law, whether produced before or after the promulgation of the Code, can be
regarded as antecedents or interpretative explanations of the
Code itself, which is the summary of his whole knowledge on
this question; although some of Bello's ideas did not become law
in the Code, such as his wish to have wills written in the testator's
own hand and, more debatable, to abolish the law whereby a
father's children have the right to a portion of the estate.[52] These
were excluded from the draft because they were rejected by the
Council of State in the discussion of the reasons behind these
ideas.

Bello did not leave to historians the task of investigating the
sources which guided him and his concordances with the
doctrines which had accumulated up to his time: the notes to
the drafts declare these in the case of each individual disposition.
The main sources are Roman law and Spanish legislation, the
civil codes of Austria, France, Louisiana, the Two Sicilies,
Prussia, Holland, Bavaria and Peru, the mercantile codes of
France and Spain in matters closely related to commercial law,
and the draft of the Spanish Civil Code by Goyena; and also the
works of many legal authors including names such as Antonio
Gómez, Gregorio López, Gutiérrez, Acevedo, Febrero y Tapia,
Molina, Baeza, Escriche, Salas, Castillo, Llamas, Donoso,
Tauri, Savigny, Bentham, Vinnius, Heinectius, Cujas, Merlin,
Pothier, Delvincourt, Portalis, Rogron, Chabot, Kent, Dodson,
Vincent, Cranch, Louis Blanc, Mathienzo, Favard de Langlade,

Troplong, Toulier, Delangle, Duvergier, Duranton, etcetera. It is a most abundant bibliography, assimilated and arranged by the scholar through long years of unhurried study.

Bello's Code has had considerable influence in Spanish America. As the Chilean Professor Barros Errázuriz has pointed out, it was taken as a model in Nicaragua, Colombia, Ecuador and Uruguay. The Brazilian draft Code by Freitas frequently quotes and praises it. The Argentine jurist Dalmacio Vélez Sarsfield, when he submitted to the Government of his country the first volume of the draft Argentine Civil Code, says that for the work he used mainly, among others, the Chilean Code, 'which is so much better than the European codes'. Manuel Ancízar, in a letter of the 10 July 1856 to Bello, asked him for several copies of his Code since, as he said, it was a matter 'of preferring to all others the legal doctrines professed in our South America, which might be a first step towards the desired social unity of our continent'.[53] Here, then, as in poetry, in international law and in grammar, we find again a reflection of the profound feeling for Spanish America which appears in Bello's works.

In Venezuela, Bello's Code was the model for the first civil code, prepared by Dr Julián Viso, who modified the first draft he had made in the light of Bello's work. The Venezuelan Code, promulgated in 1862, was in force for only a short time since it was abolished at the triumph of the Federal Revolution. Since then, French and Italian models have been preferred, and the Americanist initiative of our scholar has been abandoned. In the reform of 1942 there was an attempt to go back to Bello, in the parliamentary discussion of a draft civil code. Now and then I had the honour, in the Chamber, of invoking Bello as a still living source of urgent reforms. And in the system of private international law there was a partial, though unintended, return to the system of Bello, who 'succeeded in leaving aside the French, the Anglo-Americans, etcetera',[54] in order to seek more fitting solutions.

Bello's juridical activity was as extensive and profound as any other of the most important phases of his work. By the side of the teacher, the poet or the grammarian, the lawyer in Bello brought forth in its abundant fruit his extraordinary capacity of understanding, creativity and service.

CHAPTER 5: NOTES AND REFERENCES

1. 'There he made excellent progress in his studies and this was extremely useful to him when he drew up the Civil Code.' (Orrego Vicuña, *Don Andrés Bello*, p. 23.)
2. Amunátegui, op. cit., p. 28.
3. ibid., p. 453.
4. *Obras completas de Andrés Bello*, vol. XII (Santiago), p. x. Bello's *Temas jurídicos*, apart from the volume on natural law and those contained in the Civil Code, will appear in Vol. XV of the Caracas edition, now in preparation. This volume will contain an introduction on 'El pensamiento jurídico y social de Andrés Bello' written by myself.
5. 'Bello was the first to teach this subject in Chile.' (ibid., vol. IV, p. xxxiv.) Speech of the Dean of the faculty of humanities of the university of Chile, D. F. Vargas Fontecilla, on the centenary of Bello's birth. In Vol. XV of the Caracas edition will be printed the curriculum of this subject in the Instituto Nacional 1832.
6. *Obras completas de Andrés Bello*, vol. XIV (Caracas), pp. 477–82.
7. ibid., vol. X, pp. 19–20.
8. ibid., p. 15.
9. ibid., p. 25. He says: 'This what the Englishman Hobbes taught, among others.'
10. ibid., p. 13.
11. ibid., pp. 478, 478–9.
12. ibid., pp. 487–8.
13. ibid., vol. XII, p. 3.
14. For example, read the basic argument of his attempt to have judges give the reasons for their sentences: 'The very nature of man demands the observation of the practice of which I am writing. *Man by his rational nature* must act by the rules of good sense; and by *his social nature* must give the rest of society evidence of the correctness of the reason which directs his actions. Thus, in the greater part of the acts of our life which bear some relation to other individuals, we are obliged to give the reason for our acts or for what we say; and if there is none, these are considered to be of no consequence. . . . Why, then, in that most solemn and sacred act which is the passing of a sentence, should the judge not be asked to give his reasons, and why do we put him in the position of an oracle, giving more force to what he says than to the laws themselves?' (*Obras completas de Andrés Bello*, vol. IX (Santiago), pp. 152–3.)
15. *Obras completas de Bello*, vol. VIII (Caracas), pp. 492–3: 'Latín y derecho romano' (1842).
16. *Obras completas de Andrés Bello*, vol. VIII (Santiago), p. 311. The general prejudice against the study of Roman law is reflected in Amunátegui's *Vida* in the arguments with which this pupil 'defends' his master against the charge of being a 'Romanist'. (op. cit., pp. 346–7.)
17. ibid., pp. 387, 387–8.
18. ibid., p. 388.
19. *Obras completas de Andrés Bello*, vol. VIII (Santiago), p. 465.

20. *Obras completas de Andrés Bello*, vol. XVII (Caracas). Compilation, Prologue and notes by Ricardo Donoso.

21. ibid., vol. XVI. Arrangement and preliminary study by Guillermo Feliú Cruz.

22. ibid., vols XII and XIII. Prologue and notes by Pedro Lira Urquieta.

23. ibid., vols X and XI. *Principios de derecho internacional y temas de política internacional*, Prologue by Eduardo Plaza; and vols XXI and XXII, *Notas de la cancillería chilena*, analytical study by Jorge Gamboa Correa.

24. *Obras completas de Andrés Bello*, vol. IX (Santiago), pp. 219, 219–20.

25. *Obras completas de Andrés Bello*, vol. XIII (Caracas), p. 32. 'Human justice is not moved by impulses of revenge; its sole object is to repair the harm and avoid its repetition.'

26. *Obras completas de Andrés Bello*, vol. IX (Santiago), p. xxx.

27. ibid., pp. 193–4.

28. ibid., p. 268.

29. *Obras completas de Andrés Bello*, vol. XIII (Caracas), pp. 31, 32.

30. *Obras completas de Andrés Bello*, vol. IX, (Santiago), p. 40.

31. ibid., p. 97.

32. ibid., p. 228.

33. ibid., p. 206.

34. ibid., pp. 65–6.

35. ibid., vol. XIII, p. xxiv.

36. They will be collected in vol. XV of *Obras completas de Andrés Bello* (Caracas).

37. *Obras completas de Andrés Bello*, vol. X (Santiago), p. xv. *Principios de derecho internacional*, Introduction by Miguel Luis Amunátegui. Amunátegui mistakenly states that it was in the third edition that the title was changed. According to his quotation, Caro seems to say the same. The fact is that in the second edition (Valparaíso: 1844) the new title was used, as in the editions of Lima (1844) and Caracas (1847), while the Sucre edition (1844) reproduces the title and contents of the first. The full title of the second edition is: *Principios de derecho internacional. Por Andrés Bello, Miembro de la Facultad de Filosofía y Humanidades y de la Facultad de Leyes, de la Universidad de Chile*.

38. See Pedro Grases, *Contribución al estudio de la bibliografía caraqueña de Don Andrés Bello* (Caracas: 1944). This work is a kind of retort, or at least counterweight to the article of Norberto Pinilla, 'Bello y Caracas' (Santiago: 1944).

39. *Obras completas de Andrés Bello*, vol. X (Santiago), p. xiii, Introduction by Amunátegui.

40. *Obras completas de Bello*, vol. X (Caracas), p. 25.

41. ibid., p. 538: 'Mediación de Chile entre la Francia y la República Argentina'.

42. ibid., p. 511: 'La intervención'.

43. ibid., pp. 376, 377.

44. ibid., p. 382.

45. ibid., pp. 641, 642.

46. *Obras completas de Andrés Bello*, vols XI, XII and XIII (Santiago).

47. *Obras completas de Andrés Bello*, vols XII and XIII (Caracas).

48. *Obras completas de Andrés Bello*, vol. X (Santiago), p. cxv.

49. *Obras completas de Andrés Bello*, vol. XII (Caracas), pp. 3–22. I very much regret that it is not possible to include the message here, but its length is too great for the balance of this biographical essay. I strongly recommend its study.

50. ibid., p. 4.

51. ibid., p. 21.

52. As is the case in Rome, England and the United States, for 'in the parents' hearts the children's interests have a much more effective guarantee than the protection of the law', and 'how can one make up for paternal love if it becomes extinguished? If corrupt partiality causes a man to forget what he owes to those whom he has brought into the world, of what use are the precautions of the legislator?' (ibid., vol. XIII, pp. 187–8.)

53. Barros Errázuriz, *Curso de derecho civil*, vol. I (Santiago, 1930), pp. 46–47. The correspondence between Bello and Ancízar, in Bello's extensive unpublished letters, will be one of the novelties of the Caracas edition of the *Obras* in course of publication.

54. See the valuable study by Lorenzo Herrera Mendoza, *La escuela estatutaria en Venezuela y su evolución hacia la territorialidad* (Caracas: 1943), pp. 18–22.

6 *The Sociologist*

It is impossible to finish the survey of Andrés Bello's thought without speaking of his sociological explanation of certain problems of Spanish America.[1] During Bello's life, the social life of its peoples passed through a crucial stage. Therefore it is not surprising that a legislator, social poet, educationalist and philologist should have turned his attention to the social foundations of the facts in his view of the various problems he studied. There is no apparent sign in Bello of the idea of 'social' as it is used in connection with the problem of the redistribution of wealth and the fairer organisation of labour, which has stirred our epoch deeply in the last century. Perhaps because of the rigid and solid conservative organisation which the reigning order had established in Chile, Bello heard no echoes of the grievous problem of bosses and workers, which was already disturbing the industrial countries by the last years of his life. But rather he has been blamed for the liberal economic tone of a phrase, in which, for example, he maintained 'that in a well-ordered society the class which is most favoured by fortune is the spring from which the labouring classes derive their subsistence, the welfare of the people',[2] or the notably liberal character, in the fashion of the time, in which the hiring of labour is dealt with in the Code. But it would not be just, taking into account the time and the *milieu* in which he lived, to reproach him for not including in his works some foretaste of the social transformation which was to take place in the world as a result of the acute realisation of the labour problem.

But this does not mean that in his writings there are no obvious signs of social concern. In commenting on article 992 of the Civil Code, which reduces the rights of inheritance of collaterals to the sixth degree of relationship, he points out that this rule tends 'to divide up fortunes, and to correct one of the most serious drawbacks from which societies usually suffer, and the more so as they progress and become richer: that is, excessive inequality in the distribution of property'.[3] And in an article of 1839 entitled 'Luxury', he says that this is not what should serve 'to know if a nation is advancing or falling back', but rather 'the condition of the working class. Do we see it every day better dressed and housed? Then the society is becoming richer, and its customs are improving.'[4]

But, besides, a social interest, in the widest sense, does show in all Bello's work — at times with sharp insight, at times with marked emphasis. He has been called a social poet, and indeed social questions fill a large part of his best poems. If he is to be considered the first genuinely Spanish American poet, it is not merely on account of the lyrical tone in which he sings of Nature in Spanish America, but also because of the stress which his poetry lays on the social structure and needs of this continent.

The *Silva a la agricultura de la zona torrida* is obviously a social poem. It contains a well meditated analysis of the Spanish American rural *milieu* and a call, which is still appropriate, that we should built our life on the authentic foundations of our societies. 'Leave aside', he told the youth of Chile in his speech at his installation as Rector of the University, 'the soft tones of the lyre of Anacreon and Sappho; the poetry of the nineteenth century has a higher mission. May the great interests of humanity inspire you.'[5]

As for the civil legislator, it would be an anachronism to see in Bello's Code any traces of social concern. His provisions for the 'hiring of services', for example, can only be a reflection of the thought of his period. But a study of the form in which this contract was regarded in the various drafts of the Civil Code would be of interest. Some time I should like to undertake such a study with a certain amount of deliberation. But the Civil Code does not lack articles which reflect a concern for social justice, such as the limit imposed on the rate of interest in loan contracts, which are not entirely in tune with an intransigent economic liberalism.

We have seen how Bello's view of the codification of laws allows for the evolution of codes, which for him are not immutable instruments of a hypertrophied legal rationalism, but which should bear a 'relation to the living forms of the social order'.[6] I have told how, at his death, his copy of the Civil Code was found to be full of annotations. Because, supporter that he was of a natural law closer to that of Aquinas than to that of Rousseau, he was perfectly able to reconcile, as did Aquinas, and contrary to Rousseau's ideas, the notion of a law based on nature with the conviction of a close link between society and law, changeable to a large degree (except for the fundamental principles) according to the historical circumstances of time and place.

Bello was also able to relate the concepts of society and language. Popular usage, rightly interpreted, wisely directed to the conservation of the linguistic unity so fundamental for the Spanish American community, is in his philology the inexhaustible spring of the language. In view of this it is easy to understand his criticism of archaicisms and his defence of those neologisms which served to enrich that living and magnificent instrument of social life that is language.

Bello's work also contains clues that he did not disdain economics, that social science which was to become so important that it almost became dominant in the field of collective life.[7] For example, in his famous speech on his installation as Rector of the University he spoke of the need for the study of economics and statistics: 'The university will also study the particular forms of Chilean society from the economic point of view, which does not present problems less vast nor of less difficult solution. The university will examine the results of Chilean statistics, will contribute to their production, and will read in their figures the clear expression of our material interests.'

In his literary studies Bello also succeeded in discovering the social content of culture and made pertinent observations of a sociological nature.[8] Most eloquent is his admirable dictum that 'bodies of literature are not made by decrees nor speeches; they are the work of time and civilisation; the poverty of peoples keeps them distant, and lack of population destroys them'.[9]

But Bello's social ideas deserve special attention in his explanation of certain peculiarly Spanish American phenomena. Here again we see his balanced temperament and profound insight. From his ideas in this respect we might yet gain great benefit in coming to a precise awareness of Spanish American problems.

APPRECIATION OF THE COLONIAL PAST

One of these ideas is a revision of Spanish American views on the colonial period in order to explain the particular character of the countries. This revision was all the more meritorious since he succeeded in raising it above the passions awakened by war and stating it without fear of the clumsy slander that his call for harmony and the correct interpretation of the Spanish element of his culture was proof of his hostility to the cause of Independence.

In the thriving peace of colonial times Bello had sung the glories of the mother-land. For his first attempts at poetry he had found in the introduction of small-pox vaccination into Venezuela, which had suffered the ravages of the terrible plague, both lyrical inspiration and an opportunity to praise the Spanish monarchy. His Spanish blood was filled with pride at the victorious trumpets of the Battle of Bailén. Furthermore, traces of his devotion to Spain are to be found in the fragments which have come down to us of his *Resumen de la historia de Venezuela*.

But the War of Emancipation came. Bello would not have been human if the bloody struggle which heaped misfortune on his own country had not wrung from him emotional phrases against the enemy. What is admirable in Bello is the relative swiftness with which his judgement returned to balance, without relinquishing the common feeling of his fellow citizens. A part of the calm with which he was able to express himself on the subject of the Spanish colonisation was due to his distance from the theatre of war, but the main reason why he was able to reconcile his indisputable patriotism with historical fact was his love of truth and justice. Even in the *Silva a la agricultura*, among allusions to the 'foreign yoke', 'ancient tyranny' and similar phrases, Bello, the lover of peace, appeals for reconciliation between the brothers: 'Thou dost send us the angel of peace, to make the cruel Spaniard forget his ancient tyranny, and reverently observe that sacred, unavoidable law which thou didst give to men; to make the Spaniard stretch out to his abused brother his weaponless right hand which had been covered in blood; and if the innate gentleness is sleeping, to awaken it in the American breast.'[10]

But it was years later that he expressly rejected the insulting outcry against Spain and her colonial *régime*. In this respect, it is interesting to analyse the various articles in *El araucano* on the celebration of the 18 September, the Chilean national day, attributed by the Amunáteguis to Bello, although some may not have been his.[11] In those of 1838, 1840 and 1841 there is much talk of the 'darkness of ignorance', of the 'humiliation of poverty', of the 'colony degraded and fettered by the powerful hand of a metropolis accustomed to tame the pride of the most powerful monarchs, and which in its own decadence and exhaustion still trailed the veneration and prestige of past greatness', or of the 'dark night of depression and servility'. In 1843 there is simply an account of the festivities on the anniversary of the glorious day, the magnificent date. In 1844, the last one to appear in the Santiago edition of the *Obras completas* of Bello, the only allusion to Spain is the following:

Our present situation is certainly not the best of all possible situations; although for a people newly born, and one which has been a colony of Spain when Spain herself was not in a very enviable situation, we have no reason to be discontented with it: we should be ungrateful for the favours of Divine Providence if we were to ignore the benefits of our present state, even while making efforts, as is necessary, to improve it.

On the other hand, in 1836 Bello had recognised that 'we have had wise laws, it is true, from the time of the Spanish domination, although they required some reforms in line with the advances of the century and with our own institutions'.[12] In 1844 he reviewed the study *Investigaciones sobre la influencia de la conquista y del sistema colonial de los españoles en Chile*, presented to the university by Don José Victorino Lastarria; although in this the influence of the period is clear to see, one finds paragraphs which might have been written today when, with the disappearance of the war-time hatreds, the facts can be appreciated in their proper context. Bello worked for the re-establishment of friendship between Chile and Spain, and in 1849 (when the era of romantic history had only just begun in Spanish America), he protested in the columns of *El araucano* against a recitation which had been made in the theatre, during the festivities of the anniversary of the Independence, of a poem offensive to Spain: 'Will the land of our fathers', he asked, 'be forever an enemy land to us?'[13]

Bello's admirable remarks on the colonial past, in the study to which I have just referred on Lastarria's work, are worth reading now:

We also feel a great repugnance to agreeing that the people of Chile (and the same can be said of the other Spanish American peoples) were so deeply degraded, reduced to such complete humiliation, so destitute of all social virtue, as Sr Lastarria suggests. The Spanish American Revolution contradicts his assertions. Never has a people deeply degraded, completely humiliated, bereft of all virtuous feeling, been able to accomplish the great deeds which illustrated the campaigns of the patriots, the heroic acts of self-sacrifice, the sacrifices of all kinds with which Chile and other parts of Spanish America won their own political emancipation. And he who observes with unbiased eyes the history of our struggle with the metropolis will have no difficulty in recognising that what brought us the victory was largely our Iberian element. The native Spanish constancy was shattered against itself in the innate constancy of the sons of Spain. The patriotic instinct revealed its existence in the breasts of the Spanish Americans, and reproduced the prodigies of Numancia and Zaragoza. The captains and seasoned legions of Iberia across the ocean were defeated and humbled by the leaders and improvised armies of another, young Iberia, which, while rejecting the name, clung to the indomitable spirit of the ancient defence of the home. It seems to us to be untrue that the Spanish system stifled at birth the inspirations of honour and mother-land, of emulation and of all the generous feelings from thich the civic virtues are born. There were no republican elements; Spain had not been able to create them; there is no doubt that her laws turned minds in a completely opposite direction. But at the bottom of these minds there were the seeds of magnanimity, heroism, and proud and generous independence; and if the customs in Chile were simple and modest, there was something more in these qualities than the stupid senselessness of slavery. This is so true that even Sr Lastarria has found it necessary to restrict his assessment and make it refer only to the external and ostensible appearance. But limited in this way, it loses almost all its force. A system which has only degraded and debased in appearance has not truly degraded and debased at all.[14]

To this declaration he adds: 'If we have inherited anything from the Spaniards, it is an implacable hatred of all foreign domination.'[15]

Another article of Bello's has a paragraph about the municipal life of the old Spanish colonies, which any historian of our time would be happy to sign:

It would be interesting to follow step by step, in the light of historical documents, the life of the municipal spirit in the Spanish colonies, which the conquistadors took there at a time when it retained much of its ancient vigour in its native soil. In the century of the Conquest the Spanish American towns still displayed no small activity and zeal in the defence of the rights of the people; and if on ordinary occasions they docilely bowed to the orders and directions of the court, they did at times dare to raise their voices and even resort to arms against outrages. The town councils which led the people of the Peninsula in the War of the Comuneros bore sons who supervised the infancy of the colonies, where, because of distance, they exercised in fact a great part of the sovereign power, even electing and dismissing their chiefs, issuing regulations which were respected as laws, taking part in making war and making peace, and at times boldly opposing the viceroys, captains general and high courts. Despite the predominance of the Crown, which was extreme, that popular and patriotic spirit was never entirely extinguished in the bosom of the towns: a precious tradition, which survived the loss of its most important functions. So it is that when the Peninsula was invaded by the French armies, the town councils were seen to proclaim the rule of Ferdinand VII, drawing after them the colonial authorities who hesitated in those early days, concentrating only on maintaining the supremacy of the metropolis, whatever dynasty might occupy the throne; the town councils demanded guarantees of security from their local governors, and desired to participate in power, which finally they seized.[16]

INDEPENDENCE AND LIBERTY

Leaving behind the colonial past, Bello began an appraisal of the historical process which was carried out by means of heroic deeds; and here we find magnificent evaluations. They are not his alone: many phrases of the Liberator coincided with the distinction which Bello wrote about. But that distinction, between the Independence, or emancipation from Spain, and the search for internal political liberty, had not, so far as I know, been formulated with such clarity and precision by anyone before him. When we read Bello's sentences we find that he dissolves the apparent contradiction, with which our textbooks are filled, concerning the appreciation of the Independence as a native movement and the French and North American influences on that movement. Two objectives were being pursued at once: independence, the culmination of a natural historical process, and political democracy, an ideal spread throughout the world under the aegis of a great revolutionary movement. One thing encouraged the other; the circumstances coincided at a favourable juncture; but both ideals were often hindered, given the social conditions of the epoch. From this spring the apparent contradictions to be seen in the development of our great political transformation.

'It is not', Bello says, 'as some think, the enthusiasm for exaggerated or misunderstood theories that has produced and sustained our revolution. . . . What did produce and sustain it was the desire inherent in any great society to administer its own interests and not receive laws from outside; a desire which in the circumstances of Spanish America had become an urgent need.'[17] Which, translated into poetic language, means:

Like the lordly eagle, which no sooner has it donned its youthful plumage than it chafes impatiently against the narrow prison of the nest, and obeying the wandering instinct which incites it to soar boldly over the earth and explore the kingdoms of the air, at length launches out, and cleaves the gulfs of light; just so, my mother-land, you felt your heart beat with the daring spirit of liberty, and flung yourself into your brilliant fate; and so that immortal day whose memory today is blessed by your sons, saw you, intrepid, sublime, proud, seek the fields of glory.[18]

The occasion which allowed the nationalist desires to crystallise, or better still, the immediate cause of the realisation of those desires, was Bonaparte's invasion: 'The events in the Peninsula, which presage the dissolution of the monarchy, forced the Spanish American peoples to think about themselves.'[19] No one knew this better than the man who was in 1810 an officer in the secretariat of the Spanish Governor of Venezuela, and who in 1846 recognised that when Independence was suggested 'the rights of the Spanish Crown still retained a certain prestige, and had in their favour the concerns, the affections and the interests of a large part of the inhabitants'.[20]

But, as we have said, what is most admirable in Bello's view of the political transformation of South America is his distinction between political independence and civil liberty. The leaders of the Independence pursued two ideals: the first, which was fundamental, was emancipation, an aspiration for self-government naturally produced by the thriving state of the colony; 'a desire inherent in every great society to administer its own interests and not receive laws from outside', as we quoted above. The second was the ideal of liberty, dressed in the French fashion, which flooded the minds of the people of those days, and which reached the inhabitants of Spanish America not only directly from its source, but also via Spain herself: an ideal which Bello thought was the 'foreign ally which fought beneath the standard of Independence, and which even after the victory still had a great deal to do to become consolidated and take root. The task of the warriors was completed, but that of the legislators would not be until there was a deeper penetration by the idea which was being imitated, the idea from outside, into the tough and tenacious Iberian elements.'[21]

To Bello it seemed that the fundamental error of the patriots lay in this dual aspiration, because the two ideals were contradictory.

The Spanish Americans were much better prepared for political emancipation than for liberty at home. Two movements took place at once: one spontaneous and the other imitative and foreign, and often they embarrassed each other instead of helping each other. The foreign principle produced progress, the native element dictatorships. No one loved liberty more sincerely than General Bolívar; but the nature of things defeated him as it defeated all; independence was necessary for liberty, and the champion of independence was and had to be a dictator. Hence the apparent and necessary contradictions of his acts.[22]

There is no need to look anywhere else for a more satisfactory explanation of the phenomena which took place after the birth of these countries as autonomous entities; and this explanation is completed by this shrewd observation on the political psychology of the Spanish American peoples:

But we must recognise an important truth: the peoples are less zealous for the conservation of their political liberty than for that of their civil rights. The rights which allow them to take part in public affairs are infinitely less important to them than those which assure their persons and their property. Nor can it be any other way: the first are secondary conditions of which we take little thought, while the matters which decide our well-being, and the fate of our families, our honour and our lives, occupy our attention. Rare is the man so devoid of selfishness that he prefers the exercise of any of the political rights granted to him by the constitution of the State to the care and conservation of his interests and his existence, and who feels more injured when he is arbitrarily deprived, for example, of the right to vote than when he is violently despoiled of his possessions. If these observations can be verified in every place, for everywhere the human heart is the same, and the influences which move it are also the same, in no place could be found a better application of them than among the people who compose Spanish America. Deprived under the colonial rule of every kind of political rights, utterly blind in the knowledge of them, both on account of the organisation of the society to which we belonged and because those who dominated us took every step to prevent us from opening our eyes to the light of knowledge and civilisation, we, not considering our country to be anything else than the place appointed to us by nature in which to live out our days, must necessarily have a more lukewarm love of our political rights, that is, public spirit, than have other peoples in whom liberty has strong roots. In the days of our struggle for Independence, the exaltation produced by the revolution of ideas and the ardent hopes of a new and bright future were able to inspire in us enthusiasm enough to win our emancipation at all costs. But that enthusiasm was extinguished when we attained our great objective, and raised to the rank of nations with the same customs and the same concerns as when we were colonies; we have not yet been able to create for political rights the interest which can only be gained through knowledge of them, a knowledge which could not have been acquired, except to a very limited degree, in the short period of our political existence.

The same thing does not happen in the case of our civil rights. We have been men, even if we have not been citizens; we have had lives to defend and property to guard, even if we have lacked the right to elect our representatives. Every obstacle, then, which hinders the exercise of our civil liberty, every outrage against it, are infinitely less bearable to us than the shackles which enchain our political liberty; and the laws which protect the former bring a benefit which we value a thousand times more than anything produced by the laws which protect the latter.[23]

THE FORMS OF GOVERNMENT

Once the Spanish American countries had been emancipated there arose the problem of their organisation. Visionary theorists on the one hand, and crude and self-interested pragmatists on the other, disputed with passion. And the men of patriotic vision and heart, such as Bello, with their silence affirmed their support of sound proposals for progressive liberty which would recognise reality, but would be inspired by the purpose of firmly and steadfastly overcoming it. In London Bello was distressed by the political problems of Gran Colombia. He arrived in Chile just at the end of a period of coups and counter-coups which had led Bolívar to call it 'the country of anarchy'. He found an imperfect *régime*, but one led by men of firm patriotism. He served this *régime* with loyalty, in many of his political views he was a moderating element, but he was also able to benefit from the institutional stability which had been created, and the content of liberty which it guaranteed, in order to carry on his great work of education and construction.

Bello's analysis of the forms of government must, then, be interpreted in the light of these circumstances. We have seen that his was not the temperament of a political fighter. Perhaps also he was a little too pro-Government during his activities in Chile, although in his writings and works there are numerous cases in which he did not hesitate to raise his voice to criticise the Government and point out a better way. Bello's merit lies precisely in this balance, which he showed in other aspects of his life. In moments of democratic intoxication, when democracy was thought of more as a mechanism than as something with a basic content of respect for the human being, when men were preaching a violent transition from the colonial *régime* to a *régime* of theoretical legal equality between all citizens, unexpectedly brought into political life by the emancipation, Bello criticised those excesses and realised that the description of 'definitive' which contemporary society gave to the system of government dreamed up in the nineteenth century was fallacious.

Bello appears as a concerned sociologist in his studies of the forms of government. There is no pure form of government: 'Every government is more or less mixed.'[24] He was inclined to be indifferent about the form of organisation of the State but instead gave the greatest importance to the personal qualities of those who exercised government, whatever form this might have; and this, in that time of harsh republicanism, caused him to be regarded as being in favour of monarchy, even though he had said that monarchy could not survive in America.

For a long time we have been completely sceptical about the theoretical speculations of the constitutional politicians; we judge the merit of a constitution by the effective and practical benefits which the people enjoy under it, and we do not believe that the monarchical form, considered in itself and taking into account local circumstances, is incompatible with the existence of social guarantees which protect individuals against the excesses of power. But monarchy is a government based on prestige; its antiquity, the transfer of a hereditary right recognised by a long series of generations, are its indispensable elements, and bereft of them it is in the eyes of the people an ephemeral creation which can be knocked down with the same ease as it was set up, and it is at the mercy of the whim of the people. The time of monarchy in America is past. . . .[25] In this part of the world monarchy could only be a government of conquest, the rule of foreigners, costly to its instigators, odious to the people and ruinous to the European and Spanish American interests which, now incorporated into our present-day society, penetrate and give it life; above all it would be unstable and ephemeral.[26]

WAS ANDRÉS BELLO A MONARCHIST?

The above paragraphs show that Bello did not want monarchies for Spanish America. His clear vision saw the fundamental defects which a monarchical *régime* would necessarily have in those countries, as was proved by the Mexican Empires of Iturbide and Maximilian: In the one case the lack of a tradition to justify its forms, and in the other the foreignness of the head of state, were the decisive causes of unpopularity.

Yet there are sentences of Bello's which could be interpreted to mean that at a certain moment he did wish for a monarchy as the solution of Spanish American problems. This would not be surprising, since it was a phenomenon of a general nature. Very few of the Spanish American leaders, accustomed to the example of the Spanish monarchy, impressed by the stability of the English monarchy, and disabused by the instability of the French Republic, failed to wish, at some time in their lives, for a monarchical *régime* as a guarantee of stability in the organisation of the newly founded nations. But there is not sufficient proof to consider that Bello would have decided for the establishment of such a *régime*, and even less to allow us to assert that if he did not confess it, it was 'perhaps because he did not have enough courage'.[27] Consequently, in Chile, he never thought of monarchy.

The basic document suggesting Bello's monarchism is his letter to Mier, of which we only know the fragments transcribed by Gual for Revenga, although we have no certainty about the official labyrinths through which these paragraphs became known to Gual. The fragment is difficult to understand fully, without knowing about the other matters dealt with in the letter. It reads:

Here as you will understand the news from New Spain has caused a great pother. Everyone has an inflated idea of the advantages and resources of that part of America, and here we have now all the traders speculating. I do not know what to say of our Government, since it is keeping its accustomed reserve, although I have always been, and remain, of the opinion that our compatriots have no reason to complain of it, and that its conduct has been very different from that of that Machiavellian republic, which of all the ancient and modern nations is the most odious in my view. It is true that England, like the other European great powers, would be glad to see monarchical ideas prevail in our countries; I do not, of course, say that this sentiment is dictated by philanthropic feelings; I know very well what is the spirit of the cabinets on this side of the ocean, and I have never believed that justice and humanity have weighed for much in the balance of the statesmen; but I do say that on this point the interest of the European cabinets coincides with that of the peoples of Spanish America; that monarchy (limited of course) is the only government which is suitable for us; and that I regard as particularly unfortunate those countries which because of their circumstances are not allowed to think of this form of government. What a misfortune that Venezuela, after such a glorious fight, a fight which in its virtues and heroic deeds can compete with any of the most famous recalled by history, and leaves far behind it the struggles of those fortunate North Americans, what a misfortune, I say, that for lack of a well-ordered government (for a republican government will never be that amongst us) Venezuela should continue to be the theatre of a civil war even after we have nothing to fear from the Spaniards.[28]

At that date, the events in New Spain to which the letter refers were those connected with the Plan of Iguala, with the proclamation of the independence of Mexico and its proposed establishment as a monarchy, before the breakdown of negotiations with Spain led to the coronation of Iturbide. Which was the 'Machiavellian republic, which of all the ancient and modern nations was the most odious' in Bello's view? France, Spain and England were at that time monarchies; perhaps this reflected his private thoughts about the uncertainty of the policy of the United States faced with the problems of Spanish America. This state of mind later found a more equable outlet; but at the time it would become one more reason why, a few years later, the Secretariat of Foreign Affairs in Bogotá obstructed his desire to be sent as the Colombian representative to the United States.

Even if we admit the complete authenticity of this letter as coming from Bello, it still means nothing more than a theoretical preference for monarchy, encouraged by the inclination shown by England, but impossible in Venezuela, possibly because she was numbered among 'those unfortunate lands which because of their circumstances are not allowed to think of this form of government'. In any case, this theoretical preference did not make Bello an exception among the most eminent figures of that historical moment: because it was easy to blame the unsuitability of the system for the disorders and irregularities of political life suffered by Spanish American countries as a consequence of the war. Experience would gradually clarify his view; the failure of Iturbide, the impotence of the Liberator to reconcile the advantages of the monarchical system with the republican, would cure Bello of what he retained of this idea before he arrived in Chile; and his life in his adopted country would convince him definitively that it could evolve through a restricted democracy to a *régime* of greater liberty and that the beneficial results to which he aspired for Spanish America would depend more on the men than on the systems.

REJECTION OF DEPENDENCE ON THEORIES

For this reason Bello thought that the main defect of the legislators was excessive dependence on theories: 'Hence the short and stormy duration of some improvised institutions, whose articles are just so many deductions showing further abstract principles, or are for a people lacking in special measures which could contradict or modify them; and this assumption is morally impossible.'[29]

This is why he distinguished between written constitutions and those which truly represent the spirit of society: the former are often 'dictated by some dominant bias, or are created in the solitude of the study by some man who does not even represent a party'.

The written constition might have been formulated a thousand ways, and yet events would not have taken any other course than they did, because they sprang from the social antecedents, whereas the constitution was a passing accident. Can one describe in any other way a constitution which is greeted today with acclaim and solemn oaths, only to be spat on tomorrow? The disastrous catastrophe of Rancagua was not the effect of the written constitution but of the real constitution of the Chilean people. So when Sr Chacón tells us that only the constitutional historian who fully understands a people's way of life can show the true causes of political events, he is saying nothing that we are not inclined to agree with; but the historian who does this will not have restricted his ideas to the written constitution, but will have studied the society deeply, its customs, the sentiments which are dominant in it, which exercise irresistible force on men and on things, and regarding which the constitutional text may be nothing more than a leaf floating on top of the torrent of revolution, and which in the end sinks into it.[30]

This is why Bello also supported the need for a strong authority which would curb the excesses of liberty, as this was understood then. In my opinion, one of Bello's most important political documents is his letter to Bolívar, dated the 21 March 1827, in which Bello applauds Bolívar for having decided for 'a system which combines individual liberty and public order, better than all those which have been invented till now [he was certainly referring to the Bolivian Constitution]'.

The needs of Colombia are great; and therefore much is hoped of its most illustrious son. Among the benefits which he alone can give to his country, the most essential and urgent is that of a sound and strong government. Experience has shown that the stability of institutions, in circumstances such as ours, depends not so much on their

intrinsic excellence as on external supports, such as are supplied by
the personal qualities of the individuals who administer them. Your
Excellency's victories, talents and virtues have given you that lustre
and that command, rather than influence, on opinion, which alone
can replace that venerable patina which the centuries give to the
work of legislators. May Your Excellency continue with your
accustomed success the work of setting public order on a foundation
which, by inspiring our confidence, will make our stricken fields, our
commerce and our incomes flourish again. If all might not be able
to appreciate Your Excellency's lofty aims, if some believe that what
they call liberty is inseparable from the forms consecrated by the
eighteenth century, and imagine that, in constitutional matters, the
door is closed to new and grand ideas, Your Excellency's magnanimity will pardon this error and the success of your measures will
banish it.[31]

It was precisely his experience in Chile which showed Bello
how preferable it was for these peoples to be organised pro-
gressively, starting from a *régime* which was authoritarian but
subject to constitutional rules, rather than to swing violently
between the preaching of a political theory and the exercise of a
systematised autocracy, as was unfortunately the experience of
other Spanish American peoples.[32] He explains this position,
soon after his arrival in Chile, when he is commenting on a
message from President Jackson to the United States Congress:

Those who only see the surface of things explain the rapid progress
of the North American Republic with the single word 'federation',
as if this were the first federation ever seen, or the only one in the
world, or as if all federations had produced similar results. Any free
constitution would have been equally successful in nations with the
same natural circumstances; and the most perfect federation would
have accomplished little or nothing without the spirit which filled
that nascent society; a spirit which was born and which throve under
the aegis of monarchical institutions, not because these were monarchical, but because they were free, and in them the inviolability of
the law was felicitously united with guarantees of individual liberty.
    If in the new Spanish American States emancipation has not pro-
duced these rapid advances, the cause is easily found in a comparison
of the political education of the Spanish colonies, aimed at the single
objective of perpetuating their infancy, with the system adopted by
Great Britain in her establishments in the north, each one of which
was a free republic with a perfect representative government. What

did these people do to make themselves independent but build the dome of the magnificent edifice which their fathers had left them? We had to start tearing down, and we are still and for a long time shall be occupied in this preparatory work. But he who examines with an impartial eye what we have done despite so many difficulties will recognise that important steps forward have been taken in all the Spanish American Republics; that, in the midst of great political errors, great things have been done; that we have sustained at incredible sacrifice, and with no outside help, a struggle in which our adversary had among its helpers our own habits, our most deep-rooted concerns; that these latter are losing ground every day; that public opinion is becoming educated; that at last the time has arrived when our governments, if they wish to be permanent, have to be supported by this supreme regulator of social destinies; and (a sure sign, in our view, of the success which will crown our efforts) that the beautiful ideal of the political visionaries and the architects of Utopias has lost all its prestige.[33]

At times Bello's position was misunderstood. Otherwise it would be inexplicable that the Municipal Council of Caracas refused his last portrait, offered by General Iriarte, nephew of Antonio Leocadio Guzmán, who had recommended this to him; but it is understandable that the portrait was worthily received by President Guzmán Blanco, who ordered it to be hung in the Ministry of Foreign Affairs.[34]

In Bello's sociology reality and idealism are combined. He is neither the pessimist, chanting the praises of autocracy, nor the theoretician, forgetful of reality. He thinks about the possibility of uniting both principles and so opening the gates to the normal development of public life among the peoples of Spanish America. Above all he believes, like Bolívar, that the honesty and patriotism of the rulers are a political necessity more urgent and living than the fervent acquisition of written constitutional texts.

THE SUMMARY OF THE HISTORY OF VENEZUELA

Now we must, in this exposition of the social ideas of Andrés Bello, and as a conclusion to our survey of his thought, bring to light his observations in a work of history which has had a strange fate. This is the *Resumen de la historia de Venezuela*, whose existence – which was doubted by more than a few – was known only through a quotation of the famous Venezuelan *littérateur* Juan Vicente González in his *Historia del poder civil*.[35]

In many of his works Bello shows a deep general understanding of history. In two articles entitled 'Modo de estudiar la historia' and 'Modo de escribir la historia' his modern and balanced idea of history is surprising.[36] He also dealt with history in his *Historia de la literatura*. In his letter to Mier, discussed above, he makes a discrete complaint against 'certain declamations which do no good in the impartiality of history', since 'the memory of the events is enough to fill the enemies of our just cause with infamy; and the more surely, the more just and impartial the historian'. But among his works there had appeared no systematic historical statement of a Spanish American nature.

Juan Vicente González, a fervent admirer of his, had included as if they were Bello's a few paragraphs of Venezuelan history, beautifully written and permeated with interesting analysis; Gonzalo Picón Febres, in his *Nacimiento de Venezuela intelectual*,[37] also mentioned the *Resumen* as the work of Andrés Bello: but the critics called these citations inconceivable mistakes, because in the *Compendio de la historia de Venezuela* by Dr Francisco Javier Yanes, the paragraphs which González attributed to Bello were included *en bloc*, with a few variations.

However, a valuable investigation carried out some years ago by the dedicated *bellista* Dr Pedro Grases has revealed that the mistake was the critics'. González had inserted a genuine Bello text: and the modification which appeared in the book by Yanes showed that he used the pages by Bello, since the corrections were designed to adapt to the date of publication (1840) some phrases written at the end of the colonial period (1810). At the same time, Grases has been able to link the so-called *Resumen* of Bello to the publication of a *Calendario manual o guía de forasteros*, announced for 1809 but postponed to 1810 by the *Gazeta de Caracas*, and which must never have been circulated because at the very moment of its publication it would have been out of date on account of the revolutionary changes. That work is cited in the bibliography of the book *The Land of Bolívar* by James Mudie Spence, who takes several lines from it almost literally when writing about the colonial development of Venezuela, and which was found, thanks to the researches of Grases, in the British Museum.[38]

There is therefore no doubt that the first book printed in Venezuela was by Bello. Although it cannot be said to be entirely original, since it is rather a masterly synthesis of the histories of Oviedo and Caulin, it does condense in magnificent phrases observations on the social structure of Venezuela, at the same time as it complements and corroborates social ideas which were to appear later in Bello's writings and poems.

In fact, Bello's *Resumen* contains assessments of undeniable importance. It discreetly praises the colonising effort of the mother country, because of which 'religion and politics entered into the lists to perfect the task which had been begun by the heroism of a few men guided, in truth, by greed, but who left for posterity examples of valour, courage and constancy which perhaps will never be repeated'.[39] It praises the wisdom with which the Spaniards tried to reconcile the protection of the primitive inhabitants and the facilities and attractions which caused the European Spaniards to settle on Venezuelan soil, relinquishing the normal aim of returning to the Old World after having enriched themselves in the New. And with respect to the Guipúzcoa Company, 'to which, perhaps, might be attributed both the advances and the hindrances which have alternated in the political regeneration of Venezuela', his judgement, because it was balanced and sensible, was later welcomed without reserve by historians; because, although he plainly shows up the abuses committed by the Guipuzcoans, he also recognises that 'the agricultural activity of the Guipuzcoans reanimated the discouragement of the conquistadors and put to use, under the aegis of the laws, the idleness of the indigenous people'.[40]

In recounting the history of the formation of Venezuela, Bello places the greatest emphasis on the rural economy which was its foundation. Each of his pages is a lyric to agriculture, a forerunner of what he would later do in verse. He welcomes as a blessing from heaven (as Oviedo had done) 'the failure of the mines which were discovered at the start of the conquest', and considered this to be 'one of the favourable circumstances which contributed to give a lasting consistence to the political system of Venezuela. . . . Naturally the attention of the conquistadors was forced to turn towards more solid, useful and beneficial activities, and agriculture was the most obvious one in a country where nature showed all the ostentation of luxurious vegetation.'[41] Bello shows great interest in the system of land-holding, which was the basis of colonial development; he points out the influence of Governor Osorio, 'giving out lands, marking communal plots, assigning private holdings, giving out municipal ordinances, gathering together and subjugating to the civil order the Indians in their villages and *encomiendas*';[42] he speaks of the creative role of the missionaries in the great wealth of Guayana, and allows considerable importance to the freedom of trade established in 1778, with which 'everything in Venezuela changed in aspect, and the favourable influence of the freedom of trade was of course greatly felt in agriculture. The new system offered the landowners new resources to bring greater expansion to rural industry with products unknown in this land.'[43]

The Andrés Bello of the *Resumen*, who delights in telling of the progressive transformation of wild country into cultivated lands or of the dates of the introduction of the main crops, is the Andrés Bello of the *Silva*, whose passionate voice called on all sons of the torrid zone to turn their gaze to the fields and to honour the simple life of the worker on the land and his frugal simplicity. Throughout his exposition the same ideas occur, developed with the same poetic enthusiasm with which they were to reappear, translated into exquisite verse, in the *Silva* or in the *Alocución a la poesía*. This has been demonstrated with an abundance of examples by Pedro Grases, who, having fulfilled his task of winning back the *Resumen* for Bello, could not have completed his reasoning with a better argument. So that this scholar could not be more correct he says:

Bello's words, open and heart-felt, emphasise his hymn to the nature of the tropics, with moral reflections and a loving feeling for their fruits, in a premature forerunner of his great poem *A la agricultura de la zona torrida* and his *Alocución a la poesía*, works which would be enought to immortalise Bello's name in the history of the culture of Spanish America. In the *Resumen* appears, unripened, or as a sketch in prose, his fine poetical vision of the *Silvas*, which he was to write fifteen years later.

If in London the poem is a song of yearning, written when he was mature, 44 or 45 years old, he is yet able, while far from his country, to reconstruct and exalt the grandeur of tropical nature from the most intimate memories of his soul – heart, spirit and eye – in the early prose work he begins to weave the first literary sign of his feelings, which culminated later in his marvellous poems.[44]

The Andrés Bello of prose, then, is a rural sociologist, a lover of his country, as the Andrés Bello of the *Silva* was a rural poet. Unity in variety; soundness and harmony in the admirable fruitfulness of his life.

CHAPTER 6: NOTES AND REFERENCES

1. I must confess that I have wavered a great deal about the title of this chapter. In the first edition of this essay it was called 'The Politician'. It contained a survey of Bello's political ideas and activity. Now I have transferred the political part to the biographical sketch ('The Man'), which is Part I of the book. And in summarising here his political ideas I have decided to relate them to his interpretation of the social life of Spanish America and to his role as a historian of Venezuela. This latter section is full of interest, and there have latterly been decisive advances in our knowledge of it. Therefore I have decided to include under the title of 'The Sociologist' the exposition of Bello's social, political and historical ideas, in which perhaps my personal inclination towards sociology may give special value to what I say about Bello's notions.

2. In this case, up to a point the criticism of Dean Galdames in his book *La universidad autónoma*, quoted above, is justified. But perhaps a slower and closer study of Bello's writings might produce some foreshadowing of the social concern of our time. This presentiment is confirmed in the study of Bello's letters being carried out by the Comisión Editora of the *Obras completas de Andrés Bello* (Caracas).

3. *Obras completas de Andrés Bello*, vol. XIII (Caracas), pp. 56–7.

4. *Obras completas de Andrés Bello*, vol. IX (Santiago), p. 437.

5. O.C. vol. VIII (Santiago), p. 317.

6. *Obras completas de Andrés Bello*, vol. XII (Caracas), p. 3.

7. Thus, in his logic he makes an example of *reductio ad absurdum* from the argument that J. B. Say's principle that the value of things is a measure of their usefulness should be rejected because there are ways of reducing the price of things without reducing their usefulness, and others which make things dearer without making them more useful. This example is proof of mastery and familiarity in handling economic theories. (ibid., vol. III, p. 452, *Filosofía del entendimiento*.)

8. An observation of this sort, for example, is that because of the mutual repulsion of the social masses the Hispanic and Arabic peoples did not become united in a period double the length of that needed for Spain to become Roman. (*Obras completas de Andrés Bello*, vol. VI (Santiago), pp. 258–9: 'Literatura castellana'.)

9. ibid., Vol. XV, p. 64: 'La centralización y la instrucción pública'.

10. *Obras completas de Andrés Bello*, vol. I (Caracas), p. 73.

11. *Obras completas de Andrés Bello*, vol. XV (Santiago), pp. 335ff.

12. ibid., vol. IX, p. 212.

13. Amunátegui, op. cit., pp. 527–31. See also *Obras completas de Andrés Bello*, vol. X (Santiago), pp. xviii–xxix.

14. *Obras completas de Andrés Bello*, vol. XIX (Caracas), pp. 168–70.

15. ibid., vol. XI, p. 393: 'Expedición del General Flores' (1846).

16. ibid., vol. XIX, pp. 311–12: review of the 'Memoria sobre el servicio personal de los indígenas y su abolición', presented to the university in a solemn session of the 29 October 1848 by the priest Jose Hipólito Salas.

17. ibid., vol. XIX, pp. 454–5: review of the *Colección de viajes y descubrimientos de los españoles* by D. M. Fernández Navarrete (1825).

18. ibid., vol. I, p. 200: *Al 18 de septiembre* (1841).

19. ibid., vol. XIX, p. 359.

20. ibid., vol. XI, p. 378: 'Expedición del General Flores'. It should be noted that in the second edition of this book I attributed to Bello (*Resumen de la historia de Venezuela*) a paragraph on the nature of the emancipation as 'an inevitable event'. This paragraph is on p. 105 of the *Compendio de la historia de Venezuela* by Francisco Javier Yanes, edition of the Academia Nacional de la Historia, 1944. But the *Calendario*, found in London, contains Bello's *Resumen*, which ends with a different paragraph about the events of 1808. Therefore this phrase belongs to Yanes.

21. ibid., vol. XIX, p. 168: review of Lastarria's work.

22. ibid., pp. 170–1.

23. *Obras completas de Andrés Bello*, vol. IX (Santiago), p. 197: 'Responsabilidad de los jueces de primera instancia'.

24. *Obras completas de Andrés Bello*, vol. III (Caracas), p. 527.

25. Quoted in Amunátegui, op. cit., p. 470.

26. ibid., p. 481.

27. Norberto Pinilla, *Bello y Caracas* (Santiago: 1944), p. 14.

28. 'Una carta inédita de don Andrés Bello' in *El cojo ilustrado* (Caracas), año XVII (15 June 1908), p. 362.

29. *Obras completas de Andrés Bello*, vol. III (Caracas), p. 527.

30. ibid., vol. XIX, pp. 253–61: article 'Constituciones' in *El araucano* (11 February 1848). Collected by Bello himself in his *Opúsculos literarios y críticos* (1850).

31. Amunátegui, op. cit., p. 218.

32. In the earlier editions of this book there appeared a long paragraph from an article ('La acción del Gobierno') attributed to Bello by the Amunáteguis. (*Obras completas de Andrés Bello*, vol. VIII (Santiago), pp. 271–6.) The conclusion of our Comisión Editora, after a careful study of Bello's work in *El araucano*, is that this article is one of those which should not be attributed to Bello. The quotation is therefore omitted here.

33. *El araucano*, 14 April 1832 in ibid., vol. X, pp. xviii–xx.

34. See 'El último retrato de Andrés Bello' by Pedro Grases in *El Nacional* (Caracas; 20 September 1965).

35. *Historia del poder civil. Biografía de Martín Tovar*, by Lic. Juan Vicente González, Obras literarias, pp. 235–47.

36. *Obras completas de Andrés Bello*, vol. XIX (Caracas), pp. 229, 243.

37. *Obras completas de Gonzalo Picón Febres*, vol. I, p. 7.

38. The work in which Grases collects his early researches, and which was given a warm welcome by the Academia Nacional de la Historia in its session of the 9 August 1945, came out under the title *El Resumen de la historia de Venezuela, de Andrés Bello* (Caracas: 1946). The title of the *Calendario* (British Museum p. 1557.259. pe) is: 'Calendario manual y guía de forasteros en Venezuela para al año de 1810. Con superior permiso. Caracas. En la Imprenta de Gallagher y Lamb.' It bears notes in manuscript: 'Muy curioso': 'one of the oldest specimens of Printing in Caracas and very rare'. It consists in total of 64 pages in 32°. It has a dedication from Dr Adolfo Ernst to Sr Spence. The *Resumen de la historia de Venezuela*, s. n. runs rom p. 13 to p. 53 and ends with an account of the protests against the French in Caracas on the 15 July 1808. Another copy was found later in the library of Dr J. M. Núñez Ponte. Later, in 1950, Dr Grases published the definitive work *El primer libro impreso en Venezuela*, in which he summed up his researches and reproduced in facsimile the *Calendario*. *El resumen de la historia de Venezuela* has been published in *Obras completas de Andrés Bello*, vol. XIX (Caracas), pp. 11–55.

39. *Calendario*, p. 43, *Obras completas de Andrés Bello*, vol. XIX (Caracas), p. 44.

40. ibid., p. 48.

41. See note 39.

42. *Obras completas de Andrés Bello*, vol. XIX (Caracas), p. 39.

43. ibid., p. 52.

44. *El resumen de la historia de Venezuela*, p. 144.

7 Conclusion

In the above pages I have made a rapid sketch of Bello's ideas, bringing them together and putting them into order in a close-knit synthesis after giving a short sketch of the shape of his life and works. This methodical exposition of Bello's thought is the basic object of this modest biographical essay, and in placing it in the most vital section of this book I could find no other title for it than 'The Scholar'.

The reason, as I have said before, is that Bello was so many things: the model of the teacher, the educationist with noble ideas, the creative jurist, the man who gave laws to nascent peoples without losing sight of their social background, the nimble and subtle formulator of the principles which must rule our international legal life. He is the strong-pinioned poet, but especially excels with his close-knit vision and distilled form, the aesthete of principles, the masterly critic, the boldly revolutionary philologist, with his train of learning and his carefully purified style. Philosopher, historian, sociologist, journalist, Bello was all of these, as and when the needs of society demanded it; all in a human manner, not lacking in shortcomings and mistakes: but it would be sacrilege to name these in view of the immensity of his work. And all this was admirably balanced and noble.

In order to be all this, and to be all these things in balance; to be the source of the brilliance of the unity and depth of his broad and many-sided work, Bello could be none other than he was: a scholar of deep, of sound-training, all-embracing concern, just as were the greatest human beings who shaped the Graeco-Latin civilisation and who were its pillars.

In these times when the needs of all, and the imperative of the age, cause specialism to flourish, sometimes to the detriment of the spirit; and when specialism misforms the development of the mind, scorns the value of a humane education and the fundamental content of culture, and enslaves culture in the desperate scrabbling for material interests disguised as technology, perhaps the memory of complete men such as Bello may help to save us.

Faced with systematic utilitarianism, we must reaffirm the all-embracing and human meaning of culture. Faced with the selfish meanness whose pretext is the struggle for a living, we must be restored and stimulated by our efforts to keep alive the ideas of men such as Bello, who left their imperishable mark on the history of our peoples.

Besides, the ideas of Andrés Bello have never lost their validity. I have no intention of adopting an idolatrous position such as vitiates biographies, but neither can I regard as anything more than incidental the faults and inaccuracies that can be found in his works.

America, our America of mixed blood, is searching now with renewed faith for its road. It realises that its heaven-sent mixed blood (important only when we measure the various cultural contributions and not when we haggle over the merits of one as compared with the others), and its particular geographical situation, impose a particular attitude. In art, in literature, in the conception of law and in the making of laws; in the preservation, transformation and direction of the language; in the construction of systems of education, as in each and every one of the aspects of life in each of the fields which Bello cultivated, the Spanish Americans are trying to discover what is theirs upon which to erect the edifice of their culture as on solid foundations.

In all these fields Bello offers us his intuition and his entirely Spanish American feelings – broad and generous, with no mean hesitation, with no suicidal disregard. Of course we should study his works in the light of eternity. Andrés Bello, the model of Spanish American scholarship; Andrés Bello, with his Spanish American heart and spirit, is a magnificent example in his life and work, and in his thought is a warning which resounds in our ears and conscience. To study his thought, and lovingly mediate upon it, is not merely to honour Bello; but it is rather to honour us, the young men of the new generation of Latin America. It is to take up our heritage. It is to assume our historic responsbility which God and our countries – single in body and soul – have placed on our shoulders.

Index of personal names

Abreu, Juan José (1875–1950). Venezuelan, lawyer and Academician.

Acevedo, Alfonso (1518–98). Spanish lawyer. Author of a book on civil law in the Spanish constitutions.

Acosta, Cecilio (1818–81). One of the most brilliant Venezuelan *littérateurs*. Humanist.

Aguirre Elorriaga, Manuel (1904–69). Jesuit Father, historian and teacher.

Alfonso X (1221–84). King of Spain, called the Wise. Among his most important works is the legal collection *Las partidas*.

Alonso, Amado (1896–1952). Spanish. Philologist, pupil of Ramón Menéndez Pidal and author of the Prologue to Bello's *Gramática*.

Amunátegui Aldunate, Miguel Luis (1828–88). Chilean. Writer, historian and man of affairs. He was a favourite pupil of Andrés Bello's. Author of Bello's biography.

Amunátegui Reyes, Miguel Luis (1862–1949). Chilean. Philologist and lawyer. Continued the work of the Amunáteguis in Chile concerning Andrés Bello.

Ancízar, Manuel (1812–82). Colombian author, man of affairs and lawyer.

Argensola, Lupercio Leonardo de (1559–1613). Spanish poet and dramatist. Also prominent in public affairs.

Argensola, Bartolomé Leonardo de (1562–1631). Spanish historian and poet. He and his brother Lupercio Leonardo represent the Aragonese school of Spanish poetry in the Golden Age.

Baeza, Gaspar de (1540–82). Spanish lawyer.

Balbín de Unquera, Antonio (1841–1919). Spanish. Author of a prize-winning biography of Andrés Bello in 1910.

Balmes, Jaime Luciano (1810–48). Spanish philosopher and publicist.

Balmis, Francisco Javier. Spanish. Medical doctor who introduced vaccination into Spanish America in the early nineteenth century.

Baralt, Rafael María (1810–60). Venezuelan *littérateur*, poet and historian. A master of the Spanish language.

Barnola, Pedro Pablo (born 1908). Venezuelan. Writer, critic and literary historian.

Barros Arana, Diego (1830–1907). Chilean. Eminent historian of the Republic of Chile. Also professor and journalist.

Barros Errázuriz, Alfredo (born 1875). Chilean. Distinguished civil lawyer.

Bello, Bartolomé (1750?–1804). Father of Andrés Bello. Lawyer and musician.

Bello Boyland, Carlos (1815–54). Son of Andrés Bello. Born in London. *Littérateur* and diplomatist.

Bello Boyland, Francisco (1817–45). Son of Andrés Bello. Lawyer and Latin scholar. Wrote a Latin Grammar, which his father completed.

Bello Dunn, Andrés Ricardo. Son of Andrés Bello. Distinguished poet.

Bello Dunn, Juan (1825–60). Son of Andrés Bello. Writer, lawyer and professor. Died in the United States, where he was Chilean Chargé d'Affaires.

Blanco-Fombona, Rufino (1874–1944). Venezuelan. Author, editor and man of affairs.

Blanco White, José María (1775–1841). True name: José María Blanco y Crespo. Spanish. Theologian and writer. Emigrated to England where he made himself famous through his political ideas and his literary work.

Bolívar, Simón (1783–1830). Liberator of Venezuela, Colombia, Ecuador, Peru, Bolivia and Panama.

Boulton, Alfredo (born 1908). Venezuelan. Member of the Academy of History. Specialist in the history of painting.

Boyland, Mary Anne. English. First wife of Andrés Bello in London, who died while a young woman.

Briceño-Iragorry, Mario (1897–1958). Venezuelan. Historian and essayist. Interpreter of contemporary society.

Bulnes, Manuel (1799–1866). Chilean. General and politician. President of the Republic of Chile.

Cañete, Manuel (1822–1891). Spanish *littérateur* and critic.

Caro, Miguel Antonio (1843–1909). Eminent Colombian *littérateur* and philologist. President of the Republic of Colombia.

Casas, Juan de. Spanish. Governor of the Captaincy General of Venezuela from 1807 to 1809.

Castillo, Diego. Spanish lawyer of the sixteenth century.

Cienfuegos, Nicasio Alvarez (1764–1809). Spanish poet and dramatist.

Correa, Luis (1886–1940). Venezuelan. Author, critic and essayist. An excellent prose writer.

Crema, Edoardo (1892–1975). Of Italian parentage, he has carried out in Venezuela important work as a critic and historian of literature.

Cuervo, Rufino José (1844–1911). Colombian. Eminent philologist who left masterly works behind him.

Chacón, Jacinto (1820–92 ?). Chilean. Lawyer, writer and journalist.

Dávila, Vicente (1877–1949). Venezuelan. Historian and editor of collections of historical documents.

Domínguez, Rafael. Contemporary Venezuelan historian and research worker.

Donoso, Ricardo. Chilean. Historian. Author of many books. Has held various important positions in public and private institutions.

Duarte, Francisco J. (1883–1972). Venezuelan. Excellent mathematician. Member of the Academy of Sciences.

Dunn, Elizabeth Antonia. English. Second wife of Andrés Bello. Survived Bello.

Echeverría, Joaquín. Chilean politician and statesman. Active in the early years of the Republic.

Edwards-Matte, Guillermo (born 1889). Chilean. Lawyer and politician. Held important posts in the civil service.

Egaña, Mariano (1788–1846). Chilean. Politician and statesman, who held important posts in the Chilean Government and was also a prominent lawyer.

Ernst, Adolfo (1832–99). German resident in Venezuela, where he did important work in science and education.

Errázuriz, Crescente (Fray Raimundo) (1839–1931). Chilean cleric and historian. Archbishop of Santiago.

Escalona, Rafael (1773–1853). Venezuelan. Friar. University professor. Was remembered with special affection by Andrés Bello.

Escriche, Joaquín (1784–1847). Spanish lawyer, author of a famous *Diccionario razonado de legislacion y jurisprudencia.*

Espinal, Valentín (1803–66). Venezuelan. Printer and politician. As a master of printing, he earned the title of 'Elzevir of Venezuela'.

Espinosa Pólit, Aurelio (1894–1960). Jesuit. Ecuadorian. Eminent philologist with great knowledge of the Classical languages.

Febrero, José (died 1790). Spanish lawyer. Author of the famous *Librería de escribanos,* which was continued by Eugenio de Tapia.

Feliú Cruz, Guillermo (1900–73). Chilean. Historian, bibliographer and professor. He was Director General of Libraries and professor in the University of Chile.

Fernández y Fernández, Joaquín. Chilean Minister of Foreign Affairs in 1944.

Fernández Madrid, José (1789–1830). Colombian. Politician and *littérateur.* President of New Granada. Diplomat: died in London when Minister for Gran Colombia.

Fernández Navarrete, Martín (1765–1844). Spanish. Sailor and author. Wrote on exploratory voyages and life at sea.

Fortique, Alejo (1797–1845). Venezuelan politican and diplomatist. Venezuelan Minister in Europe.

Francisco Martín, Juan de (1799–1869). Colombian. A leader of the Independence movement, who was an executor of Bolívar and helped to preserve a part of his archives.

Galdames, Luis. Chilean. Professor, and author of books on history and education. He has been active in public life.

Gallardo, Bartolomé José (1776–1852). Spanish critic and *littérateur.*

Gallego, Juan Nicasio (1777–1853). Spanish poet and *littérateur.*

Gamboa Correa, Jorge. Chilean. Lawyer. Author of several works on Bello's international law.

Gaos, José (1900–69). Spanish. Philosopher and professor. Died in Mexico.

García Bacca, Juan David (born 1901). Venezuelan of Spanish parentage. Professor of philosophy and author.

García Chuecos, Héctor (1900–73); Venezuelan. Made a special study of the colonial period.

García del Río, Juan (1794–1856). Colombian. Politician and writer. He did excellent work as an editor and journalist.

Gil Borges, Esteban (1879–1942). Venezuelan lawyer, statesman and diplomatist.

Gili Gaya, Samuel (born 1892). Spanish. Notable linguist and grammarian.

Gómez, Antonio (sixteenth century). Spanish lawyer.

González, Juan Vicente (1810–66). Venezuelan *littérateur*, historian and politician. A great journalist.

Grases, Pedro (born 1909). Venezuelan of Spanish birth. Author and professor.

Gual, Pedro (1785–1862). Venezuelan. Politician and member of Government. Minister of Foreign Relations and a diplomatist.

Gutiérrez, Juan (sixteenth century). Spanish lawyer and author.

Guzmán, Antonio Leocadio (1801–84). Venezuelan politician. Credited with the foundation of the Liberal Party.

Guzmán Blanco, Antonio (1829–99). Venezuelan statesman. Several times President of the Venezuelan Republic.

Hermosilla, José Mamerto Gómez (1771–1837). Spanish *littérateur*, critic and Hellenist.

Herrera, Fernando de (1536–99). Spanish poet.

Herrera Mendoza, Lorenzo (1881–1966). Venezuelan. Lawyer. Professor of international law.

Humboldt, Alexander von (1769–1859). German naturalist, called the 'scientific discoverer' of the New World.

Hurtado, Manuel José (1784–1845). Colombian. Lawyer and diplomatist in England. Notable politician in the time of Gran Colombia.

Iriarte, Tomás de (1750–91). Spanish poet, fabulist and scholar.

Irisarri, Antonio José de (1786–1868). Guatemalan. Writer and politician. Representative of Chile in London.

Isnardi, Francisco (1750–1814). Italian by birth, performed important services in the Independence of Venezuela.

Iturbide, Augustín de (1783–1824). Mexican. General and politician. Proclaimed Emperor of Mexico.

Jalón, Colonel Diego. Soldier of secondary importance in the Independence of Venezuela.

Jovellanos, Gaspar Melchor de (1744–1811). Spanish *littérateur* and politician.

Larra, Mariano José de (1809–37). Spanish author and critic.

Larrazábal, Wolfgang (born 1911). Venezuelan. Sailor and man of public affairs. President of the Venezuelan Junta of government in 1958.

Lastarria, José Victorino (1817–88). Writer and politician. Pupil and friend of Andrés Bello.

Montenegro, José Antonio. Venezuelan. University Professor, who taught Andrés Bello.

Montt, Manuel (1809–80). Chilean. Politician and lawyer. President of Chile from 1851 to 1861.

Mora, José Joaquín de (1783–1864). Spanish author and politician. Worked for a long time in Spanish America. Author of important books.

Muñoz Tébar, Jesús (1792–1814). Venezuelan politician and statesman, a supporter of the Independence movement.

Núñez Ponte, José Manuel (1870–1965). Venezuelan. Educationalist and writer. Teacher of several generations of boys.

O'Higgins, Bernardo (1778–1842). Chilean. Soldier and politician. One of the great liberators of Spanish America.

Olmedo, José Joaquín de (1780–1847). Ecuadorian. Poet, author and politician. He was most important in the movement for Independence.

Orrego Vicuña, Eugenio (1900–1959). Writer, biographer of Andrés Bello. As a diplomat was sent on various missions.

Osorio, Diego de (died 1601). Spanish. Governor and Captain General of the Province of Venezuela from 1589 to 1597.

Oviedo y Baños, José de (1671–1738). Born in Bogotá. The most important historian of colonial Venezuela.

Parra León, Caracciolo (1901–1940). Venezuelan. Editor and historian of colonial Venezuela.

Paz Castillo, Fernando (born 1893). Venezuelan. Poet, critic and diplomatist.

Picón Febres, Gonzalo (1860–1919). Venezuelan. Author, critic and cultural historian.

Picón Salas, Mariano (1901–65). Venezuelan. Author, essayist and professor.

Pinilla, Norberto. Chilean. Professor, writer and critic.

Planchart, Enrique (1894–1953). Venezuelan. Writer, poet and critic. Translator from the French. Director of the National Library.

Planchart, Julio (1885–1948). Venezuelan. Literary critic and poet. Minister Plenipotentiary in Chile.

Plaza, Eduardo (born 1911). Venezuelan. International lawyer.

Plaza, Juan Bautista (1898–1964). Venezuelan. Musicologist and composer. Wrote on the history of music in Venezuela, especially in colonial times.

Portales, Diego (1793–1837). Chilean. Politician. Occupied important positions in the administration of the Republic of Chile.

Quesada, Fray Cristóbal de. Mercedarian friar who was Bello's Latin teacher.

Restrepo, José Manuel (1781–1863). Colombian historian. Active in politics during the Independence. Author of the *Historia de la revolución de Colombia*.

Revenga, José Rafael (1786–1852). Venezuelan statesman, famous for his activity in the Independence.

Rioja, Francisco de (1583–1659). Spanish poet and *littérateur*.

Rodríguez, Simón (1771–1854). Venezuelan teacher and writer. Of unsettled vocation, he travelled both worlds. He wrote works of deep observation.

Rodríguez, Zorobabel (1839–1901). Chilean. Writer and influential journalist.

Rodríguez Mendoza, Emilio (born 1873). Chilean. Writer and diplomatist.

Rojas, Arístides (1826–94). Venezuelan historian, founder of the Venezuelan historical school.

Roscio, Juan Germán (1763–1821). Venezuelan. Lawyer and politician famous for his activity in the Independence.

Rosenblat, Angel (born 1902). Naturalised Venezuelan. Philologist, pupil of Amado Alonso.

Saavedra, J. Ramón. Chilean. Author.

Salas, José Hipólito (1821–83). Chilean. Bishop of Concepción. Professor, historian and sacred orator.

Salcedo Bastardo, José Luis (born 1926). Venezuelan. Writer, historian and sociologist.

Sanabria, Alberto (born 1898). Venezuelan. Writer and journalist.

Santander, Francisco de P. (1792–1840). Colombian. One of the most important figures of the Independence. General. Vice-President of Gran Colombia. President of New Granada from 1832 to 1837.

Sanz, Lic. Miguel José (1756–1814). Venezuelan lawyer and statesman, important in the administration of the Independence.

Sarmiento, Domingo Faustino (1811–88). Argentinian. Author and politician. A man of action and a patriot. President of the Argentine Republic.

Soublette, Carlos (1789–1870). Venezuelan. General and statesman. President of the Republic from 1843 to 1847.

Spence, James Mudie (died 1878). English. Author of the book *The Land of Bolívar*.

Suárez, Francisco (1548–1617). Spanish Jesuit and theologian.

Suárez, Marco Fidel (1855–1927). Colombian philologist and politician. An eminent grammarian. President of the Republic of Colombia.

Tapia, Eugenio de (1776–1860). Spaniard. Lawyer. Followed the work of José Febrero.

Teixeira de Freites, Augusto. Nineteenth-century Brazilian lawyer, author of a draft Civil Code.

Tenerani, Pietro (1789–1869). Famous Italian sculptor. Amongst his works is the statue of the Liberator over his tomb.

Ticknor, George (1791–1871). North American critic and professor. Hispanist.

Tocornal, Manuel Antonio (1817–67). Chilean. Lawyer, professor and journalist. Statesman.

Uslar Pietri, Arturo (born 1906). Venezuelan author and essayist. His literary and critical work is important.

Ustáriz, Luis. Venezuelan. Important during Spanish colonial times, towards the end of XVIII century.

Valdivia, Pedro de (1497?–1553). Spanish conquistador. Fought in Italy, and in America conquered Chile.

Varas, Antonio (1817–86). Chilean politician and statesman.

Varela, Juan Cruz (1794–1839). Argentinian. Poet and dramatist, important in the history of Argentine literature.

Vargas Fontecilla, Francisco (1824–83). Professor, linguist and politician. Held important posts in the civil service.

Vega, Garcilaso de la (1503–36). Spanish. Poet of the Golden Age.

Velázquez, Diego de Silva (1599–1660). Spanish painter.

Vélez Sarsfield, Dalmacio (1801–75). Argentinian. Lawyer and politician. Author of the Argentine Civil Code.

Vergara, Estanislao (1790–1855). Colombian. Politician and statesman of the Independence period. Minister of Foreign Affairs of Gran Colombia.

Vicuña Mackenna, Benjamin (1831–86). Chilean. Writer, historian and politician, who wrote many works.

Viñaza, Conde de la (1862–1933). Cipriano Ostaled. Author of philological works of reference.

Viso, Julián (1822–1900). Venezuelan. Lawyer and statesman. Editor of the first Venezuelan Civil Code.

Yanes, Francisco Javier (1777–1842). Cuban resident in Venezuela. Lawyer and partisan historian of the Independence.

Yntema, Hessel E. North American. Professor of Roman law and comparative lawyer. Writer of the Prologue to Bello's *Derecho romano*.

Zorrilla de San Martín, Juan (1857–1931). Uruguayan. Politician, author and poet.

Bibliography

A la nave, poem by A. Bello.
A la victoria de Bailén, poem by A. Bello.
Al 18 de septiembre, poem by A. Bello.
Alocución a la poesía, poem by A. Bello.
América, poem by A. Bello.
Analisis idelógica de los tiempos de la conjugación castellana, by A. Bello.
'Andrés Bello, intimo', article by Luis Correa.
'Andrés Bello y Bolívar', article by Vicente Lecuna.
Andrés Bello y la redacción de los documentos oficiales, administrativos, internacionales y legislativos de Chile, by Guillermo Feliú Cruz.
'Andrés Bello y los supuestos delatores de la revolución', article by Arístides Rojas.
Antología de Andrés Bello, by Pedro Grases.
Antología de poetas hispanoamericanos, by Marcelino Menéndez y Pelayo.
Apuntes a la teoría de los sentimientos morales, by T. Jouffroy.

'Bello, el maestro inmortal', essay by Emilio Rodríguez Mendoza.
Bello, Irisarri y Egaña en Londres, by Guillermo Feliú Cruz.
Bello y Caracas, by Norberto Pinilla.
Biblia.
Biblioteca americana, journal published in London, 1823.
Boletín de la Academia Nacional de la Historia (Caracas: 1912). Learned journal.
Boletín de la Academia Venezolana. Correspondiente de la Española (Caracas: 1935). Learned journal.
Borradores de poesía, Vol. II of the *Obras completas de Andrés Bello* (Caracas edn.)

Calendario o guía manual de forasteros en Venezuela para el año de 1810 (Caracas edn: 1950).
Cartas del Libertador, edited by V. Lecuna.
Código Civil para la República de Chile, by Andrés Bello.
Código de comercio español.
Código penal de Luisiana.
'Comercio de libros', article by A. Bello.
Compendio de la gramática castellana escrito para el uso de las escuelas primarias, by A. Bello.
Compendio de la historia de Venezuela, by Francisco Javier Yanes.
Compendio escolar de la historia de la literatura, by Juan Zorrilla de San Martín.
'Constituciones', article by A. Bello.
Contribución al estudio de la bibliografía caraqueña de don Andrés Bello, by P. Grases.

Cosmografía, by A. Bello.
'Crítica a D. José Gómez Hermosilla', article by A. Bello.
Crónica de Turpín. One of the most famous apocryphal books, and the first chivalresque book in prose.
Cultura universitaria (Caracas: 1947). Journal.
'Cuna y tumba', article by Arístides Rojas.
Curso de derecho civil, by Alfredo Barros Errázuriz.
'Curso de filosofía de Rattier', commentary by A. Bello.

'De la inteligencia de los brutos', article by A. Bello.
De legibus ac Deo legislatore, by Francisco Suárez.
'De los tiempos latinos comparados con los castellanos', study by A. Bello.
De oratore, by Cicero.
Diccionario de la lengua castellana, by the Real Academia Española.
'Discurso de inauguración de la universidad', by A. Bello.
'Discurso en el aniversario de la universidad, 1848', by A. Bello.
'Discurso en el primer centenario del nacimiento de Bello', by F. Vargas Fontecilla.
Don Andrés Bello, by E. Orrego Vicuna.
'Don Bartolomé Bello, musico', study by Juan Bautista Plaza.
'Don Bartolomé Bello: precisiones acerca de su muerte', article by Alberto Sanabria.

El abate de Pradt en la emancipación hispanoamericana, by Manuel Aguirre Elorriaga.
El araucano (Santiago de Chile: 1830). Newspaper.
'El bachiller don Andrés Bello', study by Rafael Domínguez.
El cojo ilustrado (Caracas: 1892–1915). Fortnightly review.
El drama artístico de don Andrés Bello, by Edoardo Crema.
El lucero, projected Caracas newspaper, 1810.
'El lujo', article by A. Bello.
El primer libro impreso en Venezuela, by P. Grases.
El 'Resumen de la historia de Venezuela' de Andrés Bello, by P. Grases.
El solar caraqueño de Bello, by A. Boulton.
Ensayo sobre el entendimiento, by John Locke.
'Escribanos', article by A. Bello.
España restaurada, o El certamen de los patriotas, dramatic poem by A. Bello.
Estudios históricos, by Arístides Rojas.

Filosofía del entendimiento, by A. Bello.
'Filosofía moral', unwritten second part of the *Filosofía del entendimiento* by A. Bello.
Filosofía universitaria venezolana, by Caracciolo Parra León.

Gaceta de Caracas (Caracas: 1808–22). Newspaper.
Gramática latina, by Francisco Bello.
Gramática de la lengua castellana destinada al uso de los americanos, by A. Bello.

Historia Colonial de Chile, by Diego Barros Arana.
Historia de la cultura intelectual de Venezuela, by Héctor García Chuecos.
Historia de la literatura, by A. Bello.
Historia de la pintura en Venezuela, by A. Boulton.
Historia del poder civil, by Juan Vicente González.

'Indicaciones sobre la conveniencia de simplificar y uniformar la ortografía en América', study by A. Bello.
'Infancia y juventud de Bello', article by Arístides Rojas.
Introducción a la filosofía a través de la 'Filosofía' de Bello, by J. D. García Bacca.
Investigaciones históricas, by Vicente Dávila.
Investigaciones sobre la influencia de la conquista y del sistema colonial de los españoles en Chile, by José Victorino Lastarria.

Juicio acerca de la memoria sobre el servicio personal de los indígenes y su abolición, by José Hipólito Salas.
'Juicio sobre Cienfuegos', article by A. Bello.
'Juicio sobre el *Diccionario de galicismos*', by A. Bello.
'Juicio sobre el triunfo de Ituzaingó', article by A. Bello.
'Juicio sobre Heredia', article by A. Bello.
'Juicio sobre *La araucana*', article by A. Bello.
'Juicio sobre la colección de viajes y descubrimientos de los españoles de Fernández de Navarrete', by A. Bello.
'Juicio sobre los ensayos literarios y críticos de Alberto Lista', by A. Bello.

'La acción del Gobierno', article by A. Bello.
La épica española y los estudios de Andrés Bello sobre el 'Poema del Cid', by P. Grases.
'La incomprendida escala de Bello en Londres', study by Rafael Caldera.
La junta de gobierno de Caracas y sus misiones diplomáticas en 1810, by Cristóbal L. Mendoza.
La moda, poem by A. Bello.
La reforma ortográfica ante nuestros poderes públicos, ante la Real Academia y ante el buen sentido, by Miguel Luis Amunátegui Reyes.
La singular historia de un drama y de un soneto de Andrés Bello, by P. Grases.
La trascendencia de la actividad de los escritores españoles e hispanoamericanos en Londres, de 1810 a 1830, by P. Grases.
La universidad autónoma, by Luis Galdames.
'Latín y derecho romano', article by A. Bello.
Leçons de philosophie, by P. Laromiguière.
Liberales y románticos, by Vicente Llorens Castillo.

'Mediación de Chile entre la Francia y la República Argentina', article by A. Bello.
Memoria presentada a la universidad, 1854, by A. Bello.
Moisés salvado de las aguas, poem by A. Bello.
Moldes para la fragua, by R. Caldera.

Nacimiento de Venezuela intelectual, by G. Picón-Febres.

Nuevos estudios sobre don Andrés Bello, by Miguel Luis Amunátegui Reyes.

Obras completas de Don Andrés Bello, 15 vols (Chile: 1881–1893):
    I *Filosofía del entendimiento.*
    II *Poema del Cid.*
    III *Poesías.*
    IV *Gramática.*
    V *Opúsculos.*
VI, VII, VIII *Opúsculos literarios y críticos.*
    IX *Opúsculos jurídicos.*
    X *Derecho internacional.*
XI, XII, XIII *Proyectos de Código Civil.*
    XIV *Opúsculos científicos.*
    XV *Miscelánea.*
        (Prologues by M. L. Amunátegui and others.)
        Second edn (Santiago de Chile: 1930): 9 vols.
    I *Poesías.*
    II *Gramática castellana.*
III, IV, V *Proyectos de Cádigo Civil.*
    VI *Derecho internacional.*
    VII *Opúsculos jurídicos.*
    VIII *Opúsculos gramaticales.*
    IX *Opúsculos literarios y críticos.*
Obras completas de Bello, 23 vols (Caracas: 1950–69):
    I *Poesías*, Prologue by F. Paz Castillo.
    II *Borradores de poesía*, Prologue by Father P. Barnola, S.J.
    III *Filosofía*, Prologue by J. D. García Bacca.
    IV *Gramática*, Prologue by Amado Alonso.
    V *Estudios gramaticales*, Prologue by Angel Rosenblat.
    VI *Estudios filológicos I* (*ortología y métrica*), Prologue by Samuel Gili Gaya.
    VII *Estudios filológicos II* (*Poema del Cid y literaturs medieval*), Prologue by P. Grases.
    VIII *Gramática Latina*, Prologue by Aurelio Espinosa Pólit.
    IX *Temas de crítica literaria*, Prologue by Arturo Uslar Pietri.
    X *Principios de derecho internacional*, Prologue by Eduardo Plaza.
    XI *Temas de derecho internacional.*
XII, XIII *Código Civil*, Prologue by P. Lira Urquieta.
    XIV *Derecho romano*, Prologue by Hessel E. Yntema.
    XV *Temas jurídicos*, Prologue by Rafael Caldera.
    XVI *Textos y mensajes de gobierno*, Prologue by Guillermo Feliú Cruz.
    XVII *Labor en el Senado de Chile*, Prologue by Ricardo Donoso.
    XVIII *Temas de educación*, Prologue by Guillermo Feliú Cruz.
    XIX *Temas de historia y geografía*, Prologue by Mariano Picón Salas.
    XX *Cosmografía y otros escritos de divulgación científica*, Prologue by Francisco J. Duarte.
XXI, XXII *Labor en la Cancillería chilena*, Prologue by Jorge Gamboa Corneo.
XXIII *Epistolario*, Prologue by Augusto Mijares.

'Observaciones sobre el plan de estudios que ha formado la Comisión nombrada por el Supremo Gobierno en 1832', article by A. Bello.

'Observaciones sobre la historia de la literatura española de Jorge Ticknor', by A. Bello.

Oda a la vacuna, poem by A. Bello.

Oda al Anauco, poem by A. Bello.

Opúsculos jurídicos, by A. Bello.

Oración por todos, poem by A. Bello.

Orígenes de la diplomacia venezolana, study by Arístides Rojas.

Ortografía razonada, by Miguel Luis Amunátegui Reyes.

Ortología y métrica, by A. Bello.

Poema del Cid.

Política, by Aristotle.

Primera imprenta y primer libro venezolanos, by Héctor García Chuecos.

Principios del derecho de gentes, by A. Bello.

Principios de derecho internacional, by A. Bello.

Principios de la ortología y métrica de la lengua castellana, by A. Bello.

'Recuerdos de don Andrés Bello', by Héctor García Chuecos.

Repertorio americano (1826–7). Journal published in London by A. Bello.

'Resumen de la historia de Venezuela', by A. Bello.

Revista literaria (Caracas: 1865–6). Journal edited by Juan Vicente González.

Revista nacional de cultura (Caracas: 1939). Journal.

Siete partidas, by Alfonso X (the Wise).

Silva a la agricultura de la zona tórrida, poem by A. Bello.

Simón Bolívar y Andrés Bello, by Eugenio Orrego Vicuña.

'Teoría de los sentimientos morales, de Jouffroy', commentaries by A. Bello.

The Land of Bolívar, by James Mudie Spence.

Tirsis, habitador del Tajo umbrío, eclogue by A. Bello.

'Tras el Libertador político, el Libertador artístico', lecture by Edoardo Crema.

'Un capítulo de la revolución de 1810', article by Arístides Rojas.

'Una carta inédita de don Andrés Bello', article in *El cojo ilustrado* (Caracas).

Vida de don Andrés Bello, by Miguel Luis Amunátegui Aldunate.